re the

WIMBLEDON PAST

First published 1998
by Historical Publications Ltd
32 Ellington Street, London N7 8PL
(Tel: 0171 607 1628)

ISBN 0 948667 51 6
British Library Cataloguing-in-Publication Data
A catalogue record for this book is available from the British Library

Typeset in Palatino by Historical Publications Ltd
Reproduction by G & J Graphics, London EC2
Printed by Edelvives in Zaragoza, Spain

WIMBLEDON PAST

Richard Milward

HISTORICAL PUBLICATIONS

Acknowledgements

In writing this book I have been helped by many kind people. I would particularly like to thank: Cyril Maidment, Chairman of the Wimbledon Society Museum Committee, for his unfailing support, as well as for drawing some of the maps; Heather Constance and the librarians at the Merton Local Studies Centre for their great help with documents and photographs; my friends of the Local History Group for providing many useful ideas; David Heaton for reading the text and making valuable suggestions for its improvement; and last, but very far from least, Janet Koss for expertly typing the manuscript and taking great trouble correcting my many mistakes.

The Illustrations

The following have kindly given permission to reproduce illustrations:

Merton Library Service: 22, 34, 57, 60, 83, 84, 85, 88, 89, 94, 96, 100, 108, 113, 121, 122, 127, 131, 132, 134, 136, 147, 149, 151, 152, 155, 156, 158, 160, 168, 169, 170, 171, 172, 173, 182
Aerofilms Ltd: 7
Sheila Dunman: 110
Fitzwilliam Museum, Cambridge: 40
Historical Publications: 38
Cyril Maidment: 185
James Russell, St Mark's Place: 186
Surrey History Service: 9, 19
Doris West: 61
Arthur Whitehead: 13, 14, 15

All other illustrations have come from the collections at the Wimbledon Society Museum or from those belonging to the author.

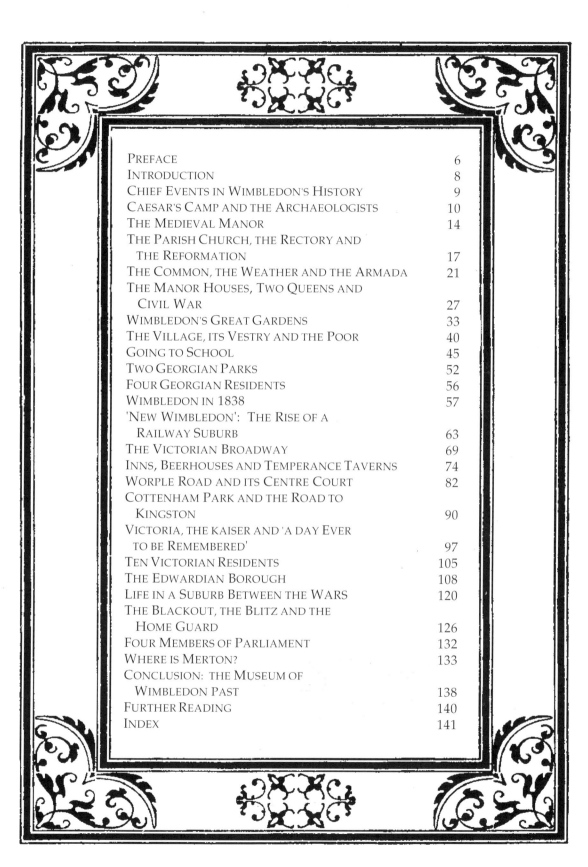

Preface

At a time when our surroundings are changing so fast, we need something more stable and permanent to cling on to. The past may not always have been very pleasant, but at least it is finished and for older people acts as a measure against which they can judge the present. Local history tries to explain that past – the people who lived then, their lives and surroundings, as well as how and why these changed. It thus enables us, as one historian remarked, 'to join a true community where past and present meet'.

Nine years ago in *Historic Wimbledon* I tried to write 'a history of all the important places and buildings that survive in the parish from the past, along with the lives of people closely associated with them'. This way of explaining the past proved very popular. The book went through two editions, sold over 4,000 copies and for the past few years has been out of print. So when I was asked by John Richardson to write yet another book on Wimbledon, I was tempted to reissue the previous history, simply bringing it up to date and correcting a number of mistakes. For a variety of reasons that temptation was resisted.

The time, I think, is at last right for a full narrative history. So *Wimbledon Past* is an attempt to write a chronological account of how the area itself developed and changed over the centuries between the building of Caesar's Camp in the Late Bronze Age and the opening of the new Centre Court shopping complex in the 1990s. It concentrates on the most significant events in the history, first of the village, then of the suburb and finally of the London Borough. It deals with people and places only in so far as they played a crucial part in that history. So inevitably there is little space for the colourful stories which punctuated *Historic Wimbledon*.

It is, however, at least as well illustrated. Illustrations are now an essential part of every good history book; they help to bring a past age and its people to life. Unfortunately, the number worth using is limited, especially for the centuries before the invention of photography. So alert readers will notice some 'old friends' turning up again from the books published in the last few years, simply because there are no alternatives. But after a thorough search of the fine collections of photographs at the Wimbledon Society Museum and the Merton Local Studies Library, a good number of new pictures have been found and are included in this history. They would have delighted Paul Bowness, the Wimbledon Society's Curator of Photographs, who gave invaluable help in finding and selecting illustrations for previous books. Sadly he died two months ago while the text for this work was still being written. *Wimbledon Past* is dedicated in gratitude to his memory.

Richard Milward
April 1998

1. *Wimbledon Common photographed from 16,500 feet by an RAF plane on 7 August 1944, at the height of the V-1 attacks. In the picture are many places important in Wimbledon's past: Caesar's Camp (an indistinct circle just off centre), Caesar's Well (a dark circle of trees to the north-east), the Common itself with Rushmere Pond (at the bottom of the picture), the Royal Wimbledon golf course (below Caesar's Camp), Westside with Cannizaro House and Park (to the right of the golf course), Queensmere (top right with the Windmill just out of the picture) and the A3 (top left flanked by modern houses). Criss-crossing large areas of the Common are the trenches and overhead wires to stop German gliders successfully landing in 1940.*

Introduction

Jean de Fleury's fine picture *A Boy Fishing* has helped to make the Windmill the best known landmark in Wimbledon. Yet in 1847 when it was painted the mill had been in existence for barely thirty years, and less than twenty later it lost its machinery and was threatened with destruction. Indeed, rather than producing corn, for most of its life it was the home of poor families living in six tiny apartments. Not until the 1970s was it fully repaired and then it was converted into a museum.

Far more important in Wimbledon's long history has been the Common in one of whose ponds the boy is fishing. Described as 'Wimbledon's most valuable possession' and, in an estate agent's brochure, as 'a place one finds with joy and leaves with reluctance', its importance has grown over the centuries and has helped to give the village its special character.

Situated on a plateau about three miles long and around a hundred feet high, the Common commands extensive views towards both London and the North Downs. In the distant past it was one of the few places immediately south of the Thames where early man could easily live. Its light gravel soil was not much use for farming, but was ideal as pasture for animals and as a source of wood. Above all, its natural springs provided a constant supply of water and so enabled people to live round its edges over the centuries. On its southern edge the first Wimbledonians built a village, farmed the land below the hill and created a small but prosperous community. Though not on any main road, the village attracted increasing numbers of wealthy and important families who built large houses round the Common.

With the creation of a railway suburb below the hill in the years after 1850, the Common became even more important. It acted as a barrier to the almost inexorable advance of London, especially after it was saved from enclosure as a park. Its fine and bracing air and lovely woodland walks have provided local people with what a writer has called 'a green lung' which gives them 'the room to breathe freely'. It is clearly one place where 'Wimbledon Past' can give hope for Wimbledon's future.

2. *A street plan of Wimbledon in 1907.*

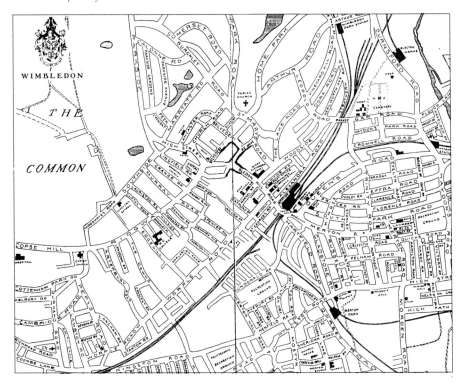

Chief Events in Wimbledon's History

Early Wimbledon

c.700BC	Caesar's Camp constructed.
c.950AD	*'Wunemannedun'* first mentioned in a document.
	Manor was owned by the Archbishop of Canterbury.
	St Mary's parish church built.

Medieval Wimbledon

1332	First list of Wimbledon's inhabitants, about 200 in all.
1437	Half the land 'wild' because of plagues.
1500	Old Rectory built by the Archbishop.
1536	Manor and Rectory taken by King Henry VIII

Age of the Cecils

1550	Sir William Cecil leased the Rectory.
1588	His son, Thomas, built the first Manor House.
1590s	He entertained Queen Elizabeth in his New Park.

1610s	He helped to organise the enclosure of a large field below the Ridgway.

Age of the Great Landowners

1700s	Cannizaro and Westside Houses built in the Old Park.
	Wimbledon House Parkside built with a large estate.
1744	Wimbledon Manor House inherited by the Spencers.
1800s	Prospect Place, Copse Hill developed into a large estate.

Growth of a Railway Suburb

1838	Opening of a railway line through Wimbledon
1850	Construction of a water main through South Wimbledon
1850s	Start of the development of New Wimbledon and Wimbledon Park
1871	Wimbledon and Putney Commons Act

Wimbledon in the Twentieth Century

1905	Charter Day: Wimbledon became a Borough
1916	Museum opened in the Village club
1940s	Blitz destroyed or damaged many houses
1965	Wimbledon became part of the London Borough of Merton

3. The Windmill about 1825, drawn by George Cooke.

Caesar's Camp and the Archaeologists

The Common has long fascinated archaeologists. From the 1750s when the Revd William Stukeley, the discoverer of Avebury, dug into a prehistoric barrow near the Portsmouth Road, to the 1990s when a man with a metal-detector turned up a third-century Roman coin, they have made some interesting finds. Near the Windmill, for instance, one archaeologist discovered stone knives used by Mesolithic hunters about 4000 BC, and on the Royal Wimbledon golf course another unearthed an arrow with knapped flint head which had been fired five hundred years later by one of the first Neolithic settlers.

Unfortunately none of these individual objects can tell us much about the early people who came to live on the Common. The one site that could possibly do that is the hill-fort known as Caesar's Camp, situated to the west of Cannizaro Park and with a fine view towards the Epsom Downs. Its nearly circular defences, enclosing a twelve acre expanse of relatively flat land, are clearly remarkable. They must have involved the moving of many thousands of tons of earth and have taken several years to complete. As late as 1865 when a local artist, F.C. Nightingale, made two paintings of the Camp, the ramparts were still nearly twenty feet high with oak trees on the top and below them a ditch twelve feet deep, quite capable of almost hiding the husband and wife shown walking round.

Yet ten years later the trees had been cut down and the ramparts deposited into the ditch. In 1870 the owner of Cannizaro Park, John Sawbridge-Erle-Drax MP, decided to develop his land and commissioned a builder, Mr Dixon, to put up some large houses along the road to the Camp. After three had been finished local people, led by Sir Henry Peek MP, raised a fund to save the Camp, but Drax would not sell the land. So in April 1875 Dixon felled the trees, levelled the ramparts and moved in bricks, cement and scaffolding. He was stopped from building, however, by the Conservators who had recently taken control of the Common. They secured a court order preventing the builder from using Camp Road for any but 'agricultural purposes'.

Caesar's Camp had been saved from becoming a building site, but was now hardly recognisable as a hill-fort. In 1907 Drax's heirs leased it, along with 240 acres once part of Warren Farm, to the

4. *A painting by F.C. Nightingale of the Camp on 1 July 1865, ten years before the trees were cut down and the ramparts levelled.*

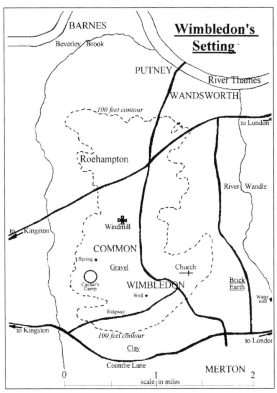

5. A map of Wimbledon and its neighbours with the rivers, high ground and chief highways.

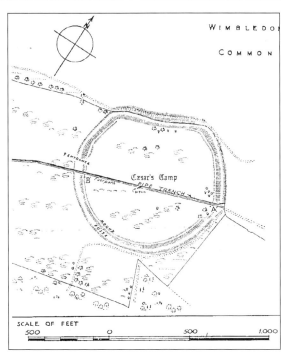

6. A plan of the Camp with the line of the trench made in 1937 and, at A and B, the sites of the only excavations that could be made by the archaeologists.

Royal Wimbledon Golf Club and, with its ditches and ramparts barely noticeable, the Camp was transformed into three wide fairways for the golfers. In the 1930s Admiral Drax threatened to sell the whole course for development, but after strong local opposition he finally agreed to dispose of it to the Borough of Wimbledon which promptly renewed the Golf Club lease. The Camp was thus secure. It was now a scheduled Ancient Monument, though every time the then John Evelyn Society put up a plaque proclaiming the presence of an old hill-fort, it was quickly vandalised.

The aura of the Camp seemed to have gone for ever. Over the centuries it had aroused wide interest under a variety of names and with very different ideas on its history. Local people simply called it 'The Rounds'. The Elizabethan historian, William Camden, knew of it as 'Bensbury' the site of the Battle of Wibbandun where the Saxon leader Cneben was killed. In the 1820s a London mapseller, G.F. Cruchley, decided to give it a more interesting name 'Caesar's Camp', as other forts south of the Thames at Farnham, Aldershot, Easthampstead in Berkshire and Keston in Kent were already (or were to be) christened. In fact,

historians now agree that Caesar never came near any of them.

A chance for archaeologists to discover the true history of the Camp came in the summer of 1937. The Metropolitan Water Board decided to lay a new main across the site and allowed first F. Cottrill and then A.W.G. Lowther to watch while its workmen dug a single five foot trench from west to east. Unfortunately the two archaeologists were not given the chance to excavate the fort thoroughly and complained that the dig was carried out 'too rapidly for careful observation'. But they did discover a complete section of the earthworks, as well as one small sign of the occupants.

They found that the Camp had just one ditch and rampart, and only one entrance, on the western side towards Coombe Hill. But the defences were still formidable: a ditch about thirty feet wide and 'at least' twelve feet deep, and a rampart probably twenty feet high with large baulks of timber on its inner and outer faces, and a palisade to protect the defenders on the top. The one trace of occupation was a small pit immediately behind the eastern bank. Inside were a few coarse pots and bowls, some containing 'pot boilers' and pieces of charcoal. There was, however, no sign of any hut, nor of any human or animal remains.

7. *An aerial view of the Camp about 1923. The near-circular outline of the defences is just visible to the left of the houses that Drax did build along Camp Road in 1870. At the top of the picture is the Windmill enclosure. To the north-west of the Camp is Caesar's Well in the middle of a circle of trees. In the bottom left-hand corner is Warren Farm. (With the kind permission of Aerofilms Ltd of Borehamwood. Negative 14201)*

With that inconclusive result archaeologists will have to be content for the conceivable future. In 1986 the Golf Club's lease was renewed for another three hundred years and the members over the next centuries will hardly welcome a new dig cutting up their fairways. Yet even the very limited extent of the pre-War discoveries has produced an interesting debate on the Camp's possible history. In his report Lowther maintained that the design of the pots and bowls shows that it dates from about 250 BC during the Iron Age, a time when the south-east was threatened with invasion from Northern France by tribesmen using a new weapon, fighting chariots. So he argued that the Camp, along with similar hill-forts south of the Thames, was a place of refuge for local families and their animals. Like the others, however, it showed no sign of any attack, and was probably only occupied for a short time.

Lowther's conclusions have been challenged in a recent book, *The Archaeology of Surrey to 1540*. Writers in this work now date the pottery much earlier, to the Late Bronze or Early Iron Age (700-500 BC). They see the Camp as one in a chain of hill-forts (like St George's Hill, Weybridge and St Anne's Hill, Chertsey) near the Thames, which were not designed as a defence against invasion, but primarily as bases for collecting and redistributing goods. At that time the river had become a main artery of trade in food and metal work, while just across the valley from Caesar's Camp was one of the main settlements where metal goods were produced, Coombe Hill. Significantly the only entrance to the Camp lay on the side facing Coombe. Its large size and massive defences could therefore have been used to protect people from the settlement along with their animals and trade goods against jealous rivals or wild animals, especially wolves and bears, numerous and formidable in the Bronze Age.

When and for how long the Camp remained in use will now probably never be known for certain. But its defences seem to have been left slowly to decay and gather vegetation – until the Victorian builders destroyed them for ever.

The Medieval Manor

THE EARLY MANOR

If the use made of Caesar's Camp is still a matter of debate, the history of Wimbledon as a whole for virtually the next thousand years is even more uncertain. At least with the hill-fort the site of a settlement is known. For Wimbledon there is no firm evidence for any permanent village before the thirteenth century.

In the past few years archaeologists, notably Geoff Potter of the Museum of London, have found traces of Norman and Saxon pottery in gardens near Eagle House off the High Street and at Claremont and Chester Houses on the Common. At Chester House there may even have been a small Saxon settlement, a forerunner of the later Crooked Billet, while near Eagle House there were signs of Norman 'industrial activity'. But these discoveries, however interesting, could simply have been evidence of a number of small hamlets, as seems to have been the case at Putney. So far no Early Medieval dwelling has been found.

Yet some kind of settlement certainly existed a hundred years before the Norman Conquest. It is mentioned in copies of three tenth-century documents. The first, a will made by Bishop Theodred of London about 950, includes the manor of 'Wunemannedun'. The second, a charter of 957, shows that its northern boundary with Wandsworth was virtually identical with that today. Finally ten years later a charter granted by King Edgar lists the manor of 'Wimbedounyng' as the northern boundary of Merton. Whichever was the original name, 'Wunemannedun' suggests that the place on its hill or 'dun' could have been founded by a Saxon leader called Wynnmann. In medieval documents the name of the settlement was given a wide variety of spellings, ranging from Wimeldon, Wymendon, Wimbledune and Wyveldon in the thirteenth century, to the fourteenth century 'Town of Wymbelton'. Our modern spelling did not appear until the 1550s and was not widely accepted for another seventy years.

Its northern and southern boundaries seem to have been established in the tenth century. Along with Beverley Brook on the west and the Wandle on the east, they enclosed a large almost square area, twelve to fourteen miles in circumference. Every so often they had to be re-marked during 'perambulations' made by the parson and some of the villagers. In the early nineteenth century

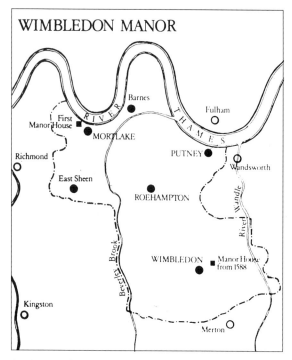

8. *A map of the Manor.*

there was a dispute with Putney over the exact position of their boundaries across the Common, a dispute that Wimbledon finally lost in 1846.

In this same year Wimbledon's days as a manor virtually came to an end. If a manor can be defined as 'land held by a lord', the then lord of the manor, the Fourth Earl Spencer, had just abdicated his rights by selling all his estate to a developer. For most of the previous thousand years, however, the manor had played a leading role in Wimbledon's history. The village was part of one of the largest manors in southern England, over 7000 acres in extent and spread over five villages – Mortlake, East Sheen, Putney, Roehampton, as well as Wimbledon (and before the Conquest, Barnes). In Domesday Book, 1086, it was entered as the manor of Mortlake, but one authority, John Blair, believes that three hundred years earlier 'the original centre may have been at Wimbledon'. Certainly, for most of the Middle Ages Mortlake was far more important with its manor house on the Thames often visited by kings and archbishops, while Wimbledon remained a mere 'grange' or manor farm. By the 1280s, however, its accounts were being dealt with separately from those of Mortlake and in the fifteenth century it was treated as a separate manor, much wealthier than its rival and so of greater value to its lord.

Ever since at least the eighth century this lord had been the Archbishop of Canterbury. He owned manors all over the south-east, including Cheam and Croydon in Surrey. Only once is there any record of an Archbishop visiting Wimbledon – in 1286 when the Franciscan, John Peckham, came to ordain two local men as priests. In his place a bailiff controlled the manor from the grange near the parish church. Most years he was able to record good crops of wheat, oats and hay from the large open fields and meadows, along with fruit and vegetables from the lord's garden, wool and cheese from his farm, and even wine from a small vineyard.

THE MANOR COURT

Village affairs he regulated with the help of a Manor Court, held three or four times a year in the church or farm at Mortlake, Putney or Wimbledon. Every tenant had to attend or pay a fine. The court agreed to changes in land holdings, supervised the proper use of the Common and dealt with petty crimes like brawls and drunkenness. It also chose local officials like the Headborough who arrested wrong-doers and the Ale-conner who tested the quality of the ale in the pubs. The decisions of the court were recorded in Latin on eight-foot long pieces of parchment, bound together at the top, tightly rolled in bundles for storage and kept in a chest in the parish church.

Along with earlier documents, these Rolls (which only survive from 1461) help to put us in touch with Wimbledonians of the late Middle Ages. A list of the inhabitants who had to pay tax for Edward III's Scottish war in 1332 has 31 names, including seven women. All must have been heads of families and well enough off to pay a fifteenth of the value of their corn, animals or goods. Allowing perhaps for fifteen other poor families who paid nothing and for an average of four to five people in each household, the total population would have been around 200, about the same as Putney, rather less than Mortlake and far fewer than Kingston. Wimbledon was still a relatively small village.

In 1348, sixteen years later, these villagers had to face the first outbreak of the dreaded bubonic plague. There is no record of the number of victims, but among them almost certainly were the two wealthiest tax-payers, Peter and Elizabeth de Spineto, as the next year their lands were placed in wardship for their son Roger till he came of age. The epidemics continued off and on into the next century and must have carried off many ordinary Wimbledon residents. By 1437 only half the holdings of land seem to have been occupied and a large area below 'the highway to Kingston' (our Copse Hill) became known as 'The Wild Land', which 'from ancient times has been arable, but for many years has become so overgrown with bramble, thorn and furze that the lord gets no profit'.

9. An extract from a manor court roll of 1703. It is in Latin (used in the rolls until about 1730) and concerns Captain Robert Knox. After an absence of forty years, much of it spent in Sri Lanka, he had come to the court to prove he was the heir to family lands in Biggery Mead by the Wandle. The entry shows that he succeeded, with the help of 'several old men that were my contemporaries'.

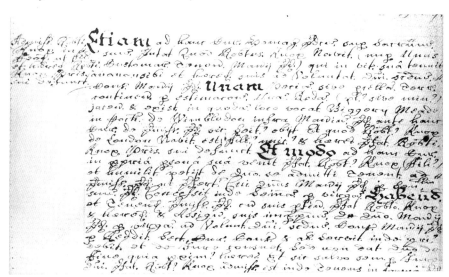

10. *Thomas Cranmer, Archbishop of Canterbury (1489-1556), who surrendered the manor, the Rectory and control over the parish church to Henry VIII in 1536.*

11. *Thomas Cromwell (1485-1540), Henry VIII's chief adviser after the fall of Wolsey. He was rewarded with the lordship of the manor of Wimbledon. His father, a Putney innkeeper and blacksmith, had moved to Wimbledon about 1510 and leased 'a half acre' in the High Street – not in the Crooked Billet as is regularly claimed in local newspapers.*

In the 1460s, as the Wars of the Roses came to an end, prosperity began to return to the village. One sign was the fierce competition between wealthier tenants for the right to redevelop this wild land. Among the richest were the heirs of Philip Lewston who at the time of his death in 1462 held an estate of over 250 acres including fields on the Ridgway, as well as land in Mortlake and Roehampton. Seventy years later his grandson, Humphrey, was able to describe himself as 'gentleman, servant unto my lord Archbishop of Canterbury', Thomas Cranmer, and bequeath his 'damask jacket, satin doublet, scarlet bonnet ... and gelding' to his heirs.

Few other tenants were so well off. The vast majority were 'yeomen', farmers who managed small plots in the common fields or were ordinary labourers who worked for others. Their lives were hard, tilling the fields and looking after their animals. They lived in small, draughty cottages. Their supply and choice of food were limited. So their resistance to disease was low. But they still seem to have been able to enjoy life.

Entries in the Court Rolls show that some even of the wealthier yeomen went too far and got into trouble. In 1465 Richard Bonham was fined for 'unjustly insulting' a fellow farmer, Robert Sawyer, and 'drawing blood', while Isabella, wife of William Wright, another yeoman, was accused of being ' a common gossip and disturber of the peace'. Others got into trouble poaching. William Bonham, described as a 'husbandman' and perhaps Richard's son, was accused in 1488 of being 'a common hunter of hares and keeps hare-hounds and other hunting dogs'.

Less than fifty years later the power of the Manor Court began slowly to decline. In 1536 Archbishop Cranmer surrendered the manor to King Henry VIII. Under Elizabeth I it passed to the Cecil family, while Acts of Parliament transferred many of the Court's powers over law and order, roads and the poor to the Parish Vestry. The Court was now mainly limited to sanctioning land deals, including the enclosure of the open fields in the reign of James I, and controlling the use of the Common. But from the start of the Civil War in 1642 even these powers dwindled, as more and more land passed into private ownership, while the rules on use of the Common were increasingly ignored. The last attempt to enforce them – by the fifth Earl Spencer in the 1860s – failed and the lordship of the manor had ceased to be of any practical value before the 9th Earl finally sold it in 1996.

The Parish Church, the Rectory and the Reformation

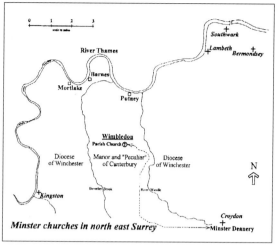

THE FIRST CHURCH

Like the manor of Wimbledon, the parish church of St Mary has a history whose origins are lost in the mists of time. No one can say for certain when the first church was built, who was responsible for its construction and why it was sited so far from the village. There is also the problem of the manor church mentioned in the Domesday Book: was it here in Wimbledon or was it at Mortlake?

The leading authority on Anglo-Saxon Surrey, John Blair, believes that St Mary's was 'clearly a relatively old-established and important estate church', which could well 'go back to the ninth or tenth centuries'. It would therefore have been founded by the Lord of the Manor, the Archbishop of Canterbury, and sited to the east of the later village near the grange or farm from which his bailiff managed the estate. It could also have been the Domesday church, argues Dr Blair, as 'the original centre [of the manor] may have been at Wimbledon'.

Behind all these unsolvable problems, however, lies a crucial event in the history of Wimbledon: the arrival of Christianity. The conversion of Surrey probably started in the seventh century, some time after St Augustine's arrival in Kent in 597, and seems to have taken a long time. It was spread from 'minsters', centres for itinerant priests who went round neighbouring villages preaching to the people and saying Mass in the open by the side of specially blessed stone crosses. Croydon was one of these minsters and Wimbledon was almost certainly one of the villages served from there, as the link between the two parishes was close until the middle of the nineteenth century.

The first church, built to enable the people to worship under cover, was probably small and made of wood. Like many Anglo-Saxon churches it would have been dark inside with low walls and small windows, cold and damp. But it would not necessarily have been primitive. Its interior walls would have been covered with plaster and painted, perhaps with religious pictures which would have glowed in the light of the numerous candles needed to illuminate the building. No trace of this church has ever been found. It is probably under the present building, the fourth on the site.

12. A map of the minster churches (marked with crosses) and the links between Wimbledon, Croydon and Canterbury. The parish should have been in the diocese of Winchester, but because the manor was owned by the Archbishop of Canterbury, its church became a 'peculiar' under the special control of his representative, the Dean of Croydon. The arrangement lasted until 1845.

The first mention in any document of the *'ecclesia de Wymbeldon'* occurs in the 1290s, during the reign of Edward I. At that very time the church was almost certainly being rebuilt in stone. It was still small and did not look very impressive, to judge from two drawings made in the 1780s just before its nave was reconstructed for the third time. But it now had a much larger chancel (whose walls partly survive inside the present church) and a wooden tower with a peal of three bells. It was also dedicated to St Mary, as were the three other manor churches at Mortlake, Putney and Barnes, as well as Merton Priory and its local parish church. In the fourteenth century it was beautified with stained glass windows, one of which showing St George still survives, and early in Henry VIII's reign it was given a pulpit for the first time and pews for the wealthier members of the congregation.

Around the church was a large graveyard. The dead were buried in shallow graves, just covered in a shroud. Coffins, like gravestones, only began to be used in the seventeenth century. Until then the graves were unmarked. So that the ground could be used over and over again, the bones of long-dead villagers were collected and placed in a charnel house, a small crypt under the chancel. As a result, the churchyard was relatively clear and seems to have been used as an open-air church hall. Fairs and markets took place over the un-

13, 14, 15. Drawings by Edwin Lessiter of three of the successive churches dedicated to St Mary the Virgin. At the top is the medieval church, probably built in the 1290s. In the centre is the Georgian church designed by John Johnson and finished in 1788. At the bottom is the Victorian church designed by Sir George Gilbert Scott and finished in 1843.

marked graves, along with plays, musical entertainments, sports and, most popular of all, church-ales where the drink was sold to help church funds.

The church was without doubt the centre of community life in the medieval village. It is impossible to say how deep was the faith of those who came to the Latin Mass Sunday after Sunday. But from their baptism to their burial they could not escape the influence of the Church with its services, its festivals and its yearly demand for a tithe, a tenth of all produce. Whether they liked him or not, none could avoid coming into contact with the parish priest.

RECTORS AND VICARS

At the medieval St Mary's this priest was often only a poorly-paid Vicar, appointed to carry out the work of a wealthy, absentee Rector. He was a man like John de Grafton in 1310, probably not very learned or much use at preaching, but capable of carrying out his main duties adequately for a congregation of peasants. His Rector, John de Sandale, like many others was more interested in gaining promotion in the church, which he not merely achieved, becoming Bishop of Winchester, but also rose in royal favour as Chancellor of the Exchequer and then Lord Chancellor.

Such clerics were only interested in Wimbledon as an extra source of income. St Mary's was one of the wealthiest parishes; its Rector could expect a stipend three or four times the average. The money came from cultivation of 'the Parson's Glebe' – large fields at the bottom of Wimbledon Hill and meadows near the church; from the villagers' tithes – a tenth of the value of their corn, wool and other produce; from the Easter offerings and from 'altar dues' – the fees charged for baptisms, marriages and burials. The revenue was sent to the Rector who only gave a small sum to the Vicar who did all the hard work.

About 1500 the Rectors began to reside in the parish once again. The reason can only have been the building of a new and magnificent Rectory. Two storeys high, with walls two to three feet thick and wings to north and south, it was Wimbledon's first brick building – and first great mansion. On the ground floor there were large kitchens in one wing, the Rector's apartments in the other, and in between a large panelled dining hall. Up spiral staircases in towers at either end of the hall were ten 'chambers' with a new type of fireplace, just introduced at Windsor Castle. Across a courtyard were stables, barns and brew- and bakehouses.

Such a mansion, far larger than a normal Rectory and more costly than even a Wimbledon Rector

16. *An aerial view of St Mary's and its churchyard about 1920. Below the church is the Old Rectory with its large garden. On the far left is the domed roof of the Well House. Above the church are the large houses in Arthur Road and the manor house grounds.*

could afford, can only have been built by the Lord of the Manor. In 1500, the Lord was John Morton, Cardinal Archbishop of Canterbury, and the King's chief adviser. Described as 'a great builder', especially in brick which was only just coming back into use in England, he had reconstructed four of his chief Palaces, including Lambeth and Croydon. His manor house at Mortlake was now old and almost certainly in need of major repair. So it is very likely that it was he who had the Rectory built, particularly as he would have been in a position to see the new fireplaces at Windsor and have them copied at Wimbledon.

Morton probably never stayed at his new mansion. He died that very year 1500 and his successors seem to have shown no interest in it. So it came by default to the early Tudor Rectors who appear in deeds living at 'Wimbledon Parsonage'. One who clearly enjoyed life there was Thomas Mylling (*c*.1522-1540). His will shows that he had a number of friends, including Bishop Bonner of London, and was waited on by at least eight servants, among them 'Richard of my kitchen'. He had also made good use of the stables, as he left

the large sum of ten pounds 'to amending the highway between Canterbury and Chatham' and so must have ridden to Kent fairly frequently.

THE REFORMATION

Such travel would have warned him of 'the King's Affair', Henry VIII's determination to marry Anne Boleyn and, if necessary, break off allegiance to the Pope. In 1534 Mylling had to ride to Lambeth and sign a declaration accepting royal supremacy over the Church. In his sermons he also had to denounce 'the pretended power of the Bishop of Rome', as well as buy a new Bible in English and place it chained up in his church. Finally, a year before his death he would have heard of the departure of the Augustinian Canons from Merton Priory and of the prompt destruction of their fine church to provide stone for Henry's new Nonsuch Palace.

Over the next twenty years there were even greater changes in the Church. First, under Edward VI (1547-53) the Reformers gained control and swept away the Mass, along with altars and most

17. The Old Rectory, with its Tudor turrets, seen from St Mary's churchyard.

18. Sir William Cecil, Lord Burghley (1520-98), holding his staff of office as Lord Treasurer.

of the old services. Then under Mary I (1553-58) the Mass and Papal supremacy were restored, only for Elizabeth I (1558-1603) to return to a moderate form of Protestantism with services in English.

The effect of such a confusing series of events on the ordinary villagers can only be guessed. As far as is known, no one in Wimbledon openly protested; all went to Matins on Sundays 'orderly and soberly' as directed by law. But their respect for the Church and for the clergy clearly suffered; those making wills left money for the poor rather than to St Mary's. It is perhaps significant that the village's only prosecution for witchcraft came at this time. In 1569 Jane Baldwin, wife of a leading farmer, was accused of 'being a common witch and enchantress', and actually pleaded guilty to killing a baby boy and the miller's wife. She was sentenced to death, but was reprieved and instead had to spend a year in prison, as well as stand in the pillory for six hours at a time on four separate days. Whether she survived the ordeal is unknown.

Over the long reign of Queen Elizabeth the Anglican Church came to be genuinely accepted, with its dignified English liturgy and its emphasis on study of the Bible. Its ministers too were better educated than the medieval Vicars. Christopher Fox, for instance, 'Perpetual Curate' at St Mary's from 1630 to 1658, was a Cambridge graduate and a good preacher. Just before the Civil War broke

out, some of his congregation wrote to the Queen suggesting that he deserved a rise in his small stipend. One lady who may have signed the petition was Mrs Knox, who was said to have had 'God in all her thoughts'. According to her son, she taught him 'knowledge of God', by encouraging him to read the Bible and say his prayers, a habit which enabled him to survive a long captivity in Ceylon.

The Reformation did not merely affect St Mary's. It also started the transformation of Wimbledon from an obscure backwater into 'a highly respectable village'. The process began in 1536 when Archbishop Cranmer handed over the manor along with the Rectory to the King. This dramatic change had two immediate consequences. The first was an unexpected royal visit to the village in December 1546 when Henry, taken seriously ill at Oatlands, had to rest for two days at the Rectory before going on to Whitehall where he soon died. Then four years later the Rectory was leased to a rising politician, Sir William Cecil, as a country retreat. His eldest son, Thomas, was brought up there and so loved the place that in 1588 he built an even more magnificent house to the east of the Rectory. The next year he became Lord of the Manor. His presence in the parish enticed other courtiers, as well as London businessmen, to settle there. Wimbledon had at last entered national history.

The Common, the Weather and the Armada

PLAGUE YEARS

The arrival at the Rectory of the Cecil family started a period of growing prosperity for the people of Wimbledon. Wills made by local farmers and their wives show they were living in greater comfort than their ancestors, sleeping in feather beds and wearing better clothes. But their livelihoods depended far more on the weather and the harvest than on the arrival of wealthy families in the village.

During the 1550s (the reigns of Edward VI and Mary) the weather was often unkind, with summers ruined by heavy rain or serious drought. For several years the harvest failed and in 1556 poor people in the north of England even starved. As a result in 1551 and again in 1557, 'the sweat', probably a virulent strain of 'flu, killed many whose resistance had been weakened by inadequate food. Among them were possibly all the members of a large family of Wimbledon farmers, the Bonhams. They had flourished in the village since the reign of Richard II; now they completely vanish from the records.

In complete contrast the next thirty years (most of Queen Elizabeth's long reign) were in the main a period of warm summers and good harvests. Inevitably not all the weather was ideal. The winter of 1564-65 was severe with the Thames frozen over and Londoners able to play football on the ice. The summer of 1573 was wet, while five years later Dr John Dee, the famous astrologer who lived near the Common at Mortlake, recorded in his diary on 26 September: 'The first rain that came for many a day; all the pasture about us was withered'. Yet until war broke out with Spain in 1585, the period was one of general prosperity, with those who survived the difficult early years of childhood living longer than their parents.

All changed again in the 1590s and 1600s. A series of miserable summers was followed by a run of bad harvests. Food prices rocketed; there were riots in some towns and epidemics of the dreaded bubonic plague returned for the first time for nearly a century. Wimbledon could not escape the infection. The parish register for 1603-04 shows that the Vicar had to bury forty or so of his 220 parishioners, nearly a sixth of the village. Over half the families mourned at least one member; some like the Lingards who ran the corn mill on the Wandle were almost wiped out.

USES OF THE COMMON

In such changeable conditions the daily use of the Common was vital for all who lived in Wimbledon. It was not a place for stretching your legs or even for airing the dog (if you had one; sadly not a single dog or cat is mentioned in any contemporary local document). Its chief value lay in its use as a grazing ground for animals. Most villagers had a cow (kept for milk rather than meat); they also often owned a horse (a heavy animal used to pull a plough or a cart), as well as some sheep (valued for their wool) and at least one pig (kept for its meat which when smoked could last for months). In the backyard they probably also had a few hens, whose eggs would vary the diet. Even a poor 'husbandman' like Henry Mayo, who lived in a small cottage on Southside in the reign of James I, owned 'my cow, my little grey nag, a red-pied heifer, my bay colt and three ewes'. Richer farmers had many more animals, above all sheep.

The competition between villagers over use of the Common led the Manor Court to try and enforce strict regulations on the number of animals which could graze there. When conditions were difficult in the 1550s and 1590s the numbers were limited; in between when harvests improved they were increased – to five cows (instead of two), two horses (previously only one), 25 sheep (increased from fifteen), while their two pigs had to have rings fixed in their noses to stop them rooting up trees. If the animals strayed they were placed in the Parish Pound opposite the Dog and Fox Inn and could only be reclaimed on payment of a fine. Fines were also imposed on all who grazed more animals than they were allowed. The worst offender was a farmer, William Brasbridge. In the 1560s he was banned from keeping any animals on the Common after failing to ring his pigs, guard his sheep and keep to the right number of cows. He seems to have ignored the ban, then moved across the Common to Roehampton.

A second important use of the Common was as a source of wood. Every tenant had the right to take three cart-loads of 'estovers' – trunks or branches of trees (mostly birch or hazel) over eight foot high. They would probably have to be found on the western slopes as the main plateau was then almost bare of trees as a result of the animals grazing there. The villagers were forbidden to sell the wood; it was for the repair of their cottages, ploughs and carts. They could also collect 'thorns, brambles, briars, ferns, furze and the like' to use

19. *A page of the St Mary's parish register recording burials in the churchyard between 11 April 1603 and 19 March 1604 (written as 1603 since the New Year then began on 25 March). Virtually all those buried between July and September had probably died from the plague. Among them were eight members of the Lingard family who ran the corn mill on the Wandle.*

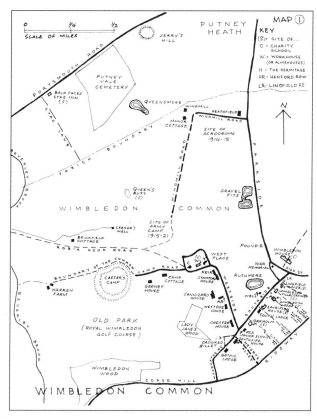

20. *A map of the common and the Old Park, drawn by John Wallace.*

as fuel or for the repair of their hedges. As with their animals, they regularly took too much wood and were prosecuted by the Manor Court especially in the 1550s and 1590s. In 1617 the first 'supervisors of the common wood' (or Common Keepers) were appointed, but they seem to have been no more successful in enforcing the rules.

The Common was also useful as a place where gravel could be dug for the repair of the roads and loam found for use on the fields to improve the heavy clay. Above all, it was the main source of the villagers' water. Springs on the western edge, above all the so-called Caesar's Well which had been in use ever since prehistoric times, never ran dry, while wells near the village produced water only twenty to thirty feet down. The best supply came from one along Southside. To protect it, in 1574 Edward Atkins was told to fence it in, 'so that the cattle [grazing round Rushmere] may receive no harm'.

THE WIMBLEDON MILITIA

By then the Common had been given a further use, as a training ground for the local militia or home guard. From the early years of Queen Elizabeth's reign all able-bodied men between sixteen and sixty were meant to train regularly so as to be ready to help defend their country. Every Sunday after morning service they had to go to the butts (probably just beyond the northern edge of the village, by our Parkside) and practise archery. The bow was still felt to be a more effective weapon than the inefficient musket. But it did need a lot of practice and Wimbledonians do not seem to have been very eager 'to have bows and arrows' or 'make sufficient butts'. They incurred regular fines as 'the butts have not been made' or 'want repair', even in the years immediately after the Armada.

Hardly surprisingly, they did not cover themselves with glory at the militia musters. Once a year, in September after the harvest was in, they were meant to go to a nearby town like Kingston or Croydon for six days' training 'in shooting at

21. *Rushmere Pond with cows grazing just beyond, painted by Elizabeth Phillips in 1838. In the background are the houses on the Green, while the trees on the right line Southside.*

a mark, in skirmishing' and in general military discipline. The richer farmers were to go as 'armed men' on horseback and providing their own weapons and armour. The poorer labourers, known as 'able men', were equipped at village expense as archers, pikemen or musketeers. Wimbledon should have been able to provide at least fifty militiamen. In 1569 they could only muster twelve, seven 'armed men', most serving by proxy, and only five 'able men', three of whom probably never lived in the village. In later years the numbers seem to have been even lower.

So when the Armada sailed up the Channel in late July 1588, the Wimbledon militia men were hardly in a fit state to help repel any Spanish landing. They had orders to be ready to march the moment beacons on Leith Hill, Betchworth Clump or Tumble Beacon, Epsom, were lit. The beacons seem never to have been fired, but on 29 July, as the Spanish fleet was being driven out of Calais by English fireships, the Surrey militia were told to assemble at three centres to defend London. The men from Wimbledon were directed to Croydon. The best soldiers, however, were sent to reinforce the main English army under the Earl of Leicester in the fortified camp at Tilbury guard-

ing the Thames estuary. There is no record of how many Wimbledon men went to Croydon, but two were certainly at Tilbury: Henry Buck, a labourer, and Thomas Pearson. Both were serving on behalf of richer villagers and neither seems to have done more at Tilbury than lose pieces of equipment. Buck had his 'hedpece' (probably a morion or helmet) taken by a sergeant, while Pearson's 'jack' (a sleeveless tunic) was purloined by an officer.

One result of the general upheaval caused by preparations to meet the Armada was the appearance of stray horses on the Common. Over several months five arrived, including a valuable 'black bald mare colt' *(sic)*. They were left in the care of responsible villagers. None were reclaimed, so they were sold by the manor bailiff.

Once James I made peace with Spain in 1604, the military use of the Common virtually came to an end – until the frequent military reviews under George III and the National Rifle Association meetings in Victoria's reign. Animals and wood-cutters regained control, with all the old offences repeated year after year. Then with the start of the Civil War in 1642, such prosecutions abruptly stopped and, apart from a few fines in the 1680s

22. Caesar's Well about 1860. The watercart has been filled to serve the houses in West Place. The invalid carriage on the left is for the crippled lady with the stick on the right. This is one of the earliest known photographs of Victorian Wimbledon.

and again a century later in the 1790s, the Manor Court seems virtually to have given up the struggle to check misuse of the Common. In 1864 the 5th Earl Spencer tried to restore order by turning it into a public park, but was defeated by the concerted opposition of professional men living in the new mansions along Parkside. In 1871 control of the Common passed to a body of Conservators. They allowed sheep and cows to graze there until the start of the First World War but their job was to maintain the plateau for 'the purpose of exercise and recreation'. The Common was therefore transformed into a haven for walkers, riders, golfers – and dogs, a very different place from the one that generations had known in past centuries.

23. Sheep returning from grazing on the Common in 1892. In the background are the cottages of West Place; in the foreground are the poles used by local laundries for their washing.

24. (Above) Wimbledon Archery Club, 1869. Two hundred years after the butts on the Common fell into disuse, archery revived in Wimbledon as a polite sport for ladies as well as gentlemen in the grounds of big houses round the Common. This picture is possibly of the Beaumont family and their friends in Wimbledon Park.

25. (Right) The interior of the Cecil chapel in the parish church. Sir Edward Cecil, Viscount Wimbledon, had the chapel built and was himself buried in the black marble tomb in 1638. The plaques and coats of arms in the little windows commemorate his daughters. On the wall, when this photograph was taken in 1921, were helmets and pieces of armour worn by infantrymen in the 1630s. All, along with the coronet over the tomb, have since been stolen.

The Manor Houses, Two Queens and Civil War

THE ELIZABETHAN HOUSE

The preservation of the Common was one of the great achievements of our Victorian ancestors. In sad contrast the complete obliteration of Wimbledon's first and finest manor house must be one of the worst decisions of their Georgian predecessors. The building was pulled down in the 1720s and its site landscaped to create a northern vista from the Duchess of Marlborough's new house. Forty years later further damage was done when a large embankment was created there by 'Capability' Brown. So in 1992, when members of the Wimbledon Society tried to trace the Elizabethan foundations, all they could find were a few Tudor bricks – and many pieces of medieval pottery. Even the floors of the basement which had been sunk into the hillside had vanished. Yet if the house had survived, it would now be a major attraction, overlooking the All-England Lawn Tennis Club.

It had been built in the year of the Armada, as the ominous date '1588' over the gate reminded Count Gondomar, the Spanish Ambassador, on a visit to the house thirty years later. Its creator was Sir Thomas Cecil, the eldest son of Lord Burghley, the Queen's trusted adviser, yet capable of showing no 'fatherly affection' to a son who preferred sport and fighting to study and hard work. Since 1575 Thomas had been living happily at the Rectory with his wife and their thirteen children. He had grown to love Wimbledon and decided to build here a new and even grander house, one to rival his father's mansions at Burghley and Theobalds. He hoped thus to create one of the great 'prestige houses' in Elizabethan England and so both assert his importance and entice the

26. A map showing the position of the four Wimbledon manor houses.

27. Thomas Cecil, Earl of Exeter (1542-1623).

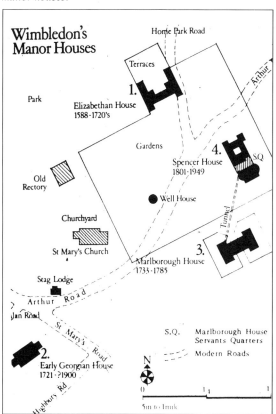

28. *The front of the Elizabethan manor house as seen from the park; drawn by Henry Winstanley in 1678.*

Queen to pay him a state visit.

Sadly all documents recording its building seem to have vanished. They may have been lost when in 1628 part of the house was blown up 'by the mistaking of some maids who, instead of a barrel of soap, opened a barrel of gunpowder which lay in the cellar and let a spark of the candle fall in'. We therefore have no idea how much it cost, nor how long it took to build. The name of the architect is also not recorded, though doubtless Thomas played a part in the design. Whoever he was, the architect included two novel ideas in his plan. First, instead of the traditional 'E' shape with two wings and a protruding central door, he used 'a truncated H' with the wings also projecting slightly backwards towards the garden. Even more dramatically he made the main approach to the house from the north through the new park, reaching the front door up a series of terraces (an idea perhaps borrowed from a Farnese palace north of Rome). Though only two storeys high, the house was built of 'excellent good brick' with expensive stone used just for the quoins, and seemed to dominate the area because of its position on the slope of the hill and its twin towers containing the staircases. Without these advantages the garden front looked far less striking.

29. Thomas Cecil's son, Edward, Viscount Wimbledon (1571-1638).

The interior was said to be 'very rich'. Just inside the front door was 'a fair and large hall' for banquets and great occasions, with state rooms beyond decorated with black and white marble floors, elaborate fireplaces and panelled walls. Up the main staircase, hung with paintings, was 'a great gallery' which ran the length of the north front and gave fine views over the park. Opening off it were rooms facing the gardens – 'a fair dining room', 'a great chamber' and the family bedrooms. Above in the gables was 'Mr Cecil's chamber', a nursery, 'a great drying room', a large lead cistern (the main water-supply) and a clock tower. Below in the basement lived an army of servants – the steward, cooks, maids and menservants – surrounded by 'the spacious kitchens' and a large array of store-rooms.

The house impressed contemporaries. William Camden, the famous Elizabethan historian, described it as 'Wimbledon's greatest ornament'. Thomas Fuller, author of *The Worthies of England*, declared it was 'a daring structure'. But the highest praise came from the Parliamentary commissioners who surveyed it in 1649: 'We find the site very pleasant, the rooms richly adorned and commodious, the air sweet and open, the church and market near, and the convenience and nearness of London of no small advantage, the gardens richly planted, being a seat of a large prospect'.

Such an impressive mansion quickly won Cecil the Queen's favour. Though she had been lord of the manor ever since her accession, Elizabeth had made no move to visit it – until she disposed of the lordship to Cecil in 1589 and he had built a house worthy to receive her. In the 1590s therefore she paid at least three, possibly four visits to Wimbledon. The most notable came in 1599. It was part of a great progress, starting from Greenwich Palace and going through Surrey, Hampshire and Berkshire to end at Windsor Castle. As with all the Queen's summer tours, it involved careful preparation and considerable expense for those honoured with a visit, as a large number of courtiers came too and had to be fed and entertained. Unfortunately on this occasion Elizabeth, now well into her sixties, was even more indecisive than usual. She kept on changing the date for the start of the progress, with disastrous consequences for her hosts. Thomas got so annoyed that he wrote to his half-brother Robert, the Secretary of State: 'Her Majesty's coming and not coming so distempers all things with me, as upon every change I do nothing but give directions into the country for new provisions; most of the old have had to be thrown away by reason of the heat'. In the end the Queen did come, two weeks late. She was given a great formal welcome on the terraces in front of the house and was then entertained with a banquet and probably a hunt in the park. She stayed three days. Shortly after she left Cecil gained his reward – his first major office of state as Lord President of the Council of the North.

Under King James I he continued to prosper – made first a Privy Councillor, then an Earl (apparently choosing the title Exeter for no other reason than that no one else held it). His new manor house was visited by the King on several occasions. In 1616, for instance, James who loved hunting 'killed a brace of stags' before dinner. By then Cecil was well into his seventies and crippled with gout. On his death in 1623, he left Wimbledon manor to his third son Edward, a brave soldier who was made Viscount Wimbledon by Charles I despite leading a disastrous attack on Cadiz. His supreme ambition was to have a son and heir, but the long-awaited boy only survived a few months. Not long afterwards the father himself died and was buried in a special chapel at St Mary's church under a handsome black marble tomb. In his will he left the estate to his four daughters. Three were already married to wealthy landowners and were living elsewhere. So they agreed to sell the house and park.

In 1639 the two were bought for £16,789 (an intriguing figure) by the King, even though he was already having serious trouble raising money for war with the Scots. He secured it for his wife, Henrietta Maria. She already held several manors west of London, but seems to have wanted another one, either for her mother, Marie de Medici, who had just arrived in England, or as a country retreat for the royal children. She therefore insisted on major alterations to the house. The leading architect, Inigo Jones, was employed to add royal apartments facing the garden. They were provided with a new water system and a bathroom (the first in Wimbledon). The fireplaces were modernised, new 'freeses' were put up and paintings by Rubens and Van Dyck hung on the walls. Almost certainly the King and Queen came to see the work, though there is no documentary proof that they did so. After three years, however, the improvements were still unfinished and there they had to stay, as early in 1642 the royal family decided to leave London.

THE CIVIL WAR

On the outbreak of Civil War that August Wimbledon house and park were left in the care of Henrietta's Treasurer, Sir Richard Wynn. He shut up as much of the house as possible, including a room 'wherein the pictures are' under 'lock and

30. Sir Richard Wynn (1588-1649) who looked after the manor house during the Civil War.

key'. He also had to dismiss over half the servants, including the laundry maids who were no longer needed. But he kept up repairs to the building, maintained some heat in the rooms with regular sacks of 'charcoles' and above all looked after the gardens and the park, providing food for the swans and the deer.

Sir Richard's chief headache, however, was the protection of both house and park. Henrietta was a noted 'Papist' and very unpopular. So there was always a chance that unruly soldiers or a crowd of Londoners would attack her property. The Treasurer, therefore, promptly bought six halberds 'for Her Majesty's service at Wimbledon' and later added two bows and some arrows. But these proved no deterrent for 'troopers' who 'threw over' the palings round the park, stole wood and tried to poach the deer. Even after the war officially ended in 1646, his troubles did not stop. He had to billet soldiers in the house, secure the arrest of those who killed his 'genny henns' and ask the Commander of the New Model Army, Sir Thomas Fairfax, 'for a protection for the preservation of Wimbledon park and house'. Despite this, the house was burgled and some of his wife's property stolen, and he even had to summon soldiers from Chelsea 'to take them that destroyed the [fish] ponds' in the park.

Worn out by all these worries and the general uncertainty, Sir Richard died in July 1649, less than six months after his King had been executed in Whitehall. He was buried in St Mary's; his gravestone is still there just below the gate into the chancel. A few weeks later Colonel Wilson and a troop of soldiers 'took possession of Wimbledon Park House and gardens'. They were followed by Colonel Webb and 'the surveyors of the County of Surrey' who produced a detailed report on the entire property and assessed its value very exactly at £9,452. A year later it was sold for £16,825, almost exactly the sum Henrietta had paid for it, and quickly resold at a profit of £3,000 to one of the leading generals, John Lambert.

LATER MANOR HOUSES

The Elizabethan manor house survived another seventy years, long enough to have two fine drawings made of it by Henry Winstanley in 1678. By the reign of George I it was in need of repair and its style was considered out of date. So in 1720 it was pulled down. It was succeeded by three further manor houses – Belvedere House, which survived as a private house until 1900, the Duchess of Marlborough's House, which was burnt out in 1785, and the Spencer House, which was itself pulled down in 1949. Now the only surviving building from Wimbledon's manorial past is the Well House in Arthur Road, built by Earl Spencer in 1798, but now transformed into a delightful private residence.

31. Lieutenant-General John Lambert (1619-84).

32. A model of the Marlborough Manor House, in the Wimbledon Museum.

33. The front of Belvedere House (originally the second manor house), drawn by G. Prosser in 1828.

35. The south front of the Spencer House, drawn by William Porden about 1815.

34. The Pageant held in the grounds of Wimbledon Park House in June 1925. A large crowd watch one of 'the incidents of the past of Wimbledon'. Queen Elizabeth I (played by Mrs Montgomery-Williams) under a canopy leading her courtiers in 1597 to meet Lord Burghley (Mr R.C. Botwright).

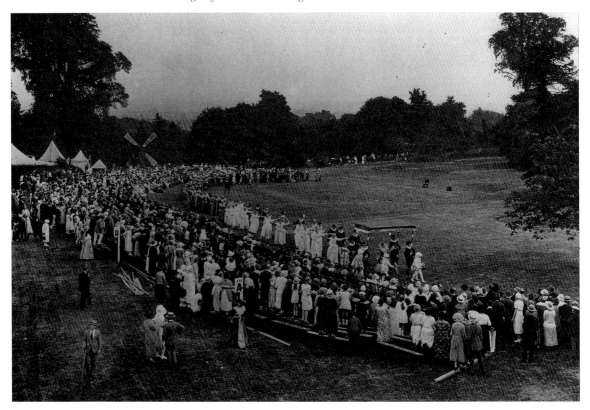

Wimbledon's Great Gardens

THE MANOR HOUSE GARDENS

Sir Thomas Cecil's manor house certainly made Wimbledon known at Court and in the City. But almost as important was the twenty-acre garden that stretched up the slope behind the house onto the plateau (where Arthur Road runs today). It was not the first garden known in the village. The medieval manor bailiff had one at his grange near the church; in 1236 he had it dug and planted with flowers. The Tudor Rectory too had a garden with an orchard, two dovecots and a summer house. In the 1550s Sir William Cecil, a keen gardener, had red roses sent from London probably to plant there, followed later by orange and lemon trees.

The Elizabethan garden, however, was on a far grander scale. Like the house, it was a 'prestige project', very large and formal, based on Italian models and enclosed in a high brick wall. Cecil took over twenty years to complete the final layout. A plan, drawn in 1609 by the architect, Robert Smythson, shows the garden still unfinished with 'a great orchard now being planted'. The earliest part near the house consisted of a number of small gardens, bounded by walls or hedges. In them were flowers, especially roses, or else herbs, or apple, cherry and pear trees, along with fountains, low box hedges and gravel walks. Later the garden was expanded up the hill with a lime walk, noted 'for both shade and sweetness', a large orchard and at the top a vineyard which does not seem to have lasted long, perhaps killed off in the severe winter of 1635.

Shortly afterwards the garden like the house underwent major changes ordered by its new owner, Queen Henrietta Maria. Brought up at the French Court where a more symmetrical style was the fashion, she wanted her garden designed in the same way. So she engaged André Mollet, the leading French gardener who had earlier laid out the gardens at St James's Palace. He swept away the rather muddled line of small gardens near the house and replaced them with square terrace gardens, adorned with cypress trees, box hedges and fountains, and a central vista up steps to the lime walk. On the eastern side of the house he created an 'orange garden' with sixty orange trees imported from Holland just before the Civil War, planted in tubs and kept in a covered loggia during the winter. At the top of the plateau he replaced the vineyard with a maze and 'a wilderness –

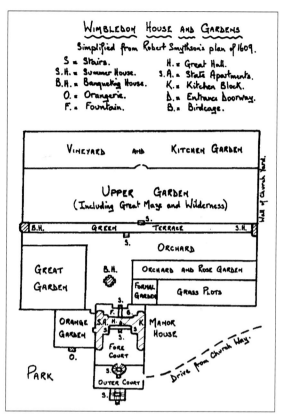

36. A simplified version of Smythson's plan of the manor house garden in 1609.

plantations of young trees, formed into ovals, squares and angles'.

So much time and money had been spent on the garden that even during the Civil War Henrietta's Treasurer, Sir Richard Wynn, felt it had to be properly maintained. So he retained one of the French gardeners, Laurence Coussin, helped by an English under-gardener. He also regularly employed a number of local men and women to dig the beds and do the weeding, while he provided traps and shot to catch moles and kill 'the jayes and other birds which spoil the gardens'.

Consequently when in 1652 the Cromwellian General, John Lambert, moved into the manor house, he found that its gardens had been well looked after. Like his predecessors he was a keen gardener and had his own ideas on the layout. Instead of following Italian or French models, he preferred the Dutch practice of planting a lot of flowers. He therefore brought in many plants from abroad, notably the Guernsey lily and the tulip. His love of this flower led Royalist satirists to dub him 'Knight of the Golden Tulip'. His stay

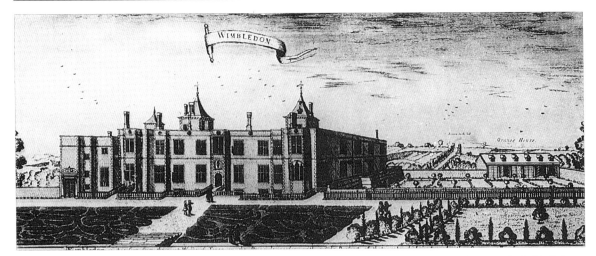

37.   Winstanley's drawing of the south front made 'from the great walke of trees in the principle garden'. Behind the 'orange house' on the right lay the park with its tree-lined drive.

in Wimbledon, however, was short. With the Restoration of Charles II in 1660, he was imprisoned in Guernsey and the manor passed in turn to two leading Royalists – George Digby, Earl of Bristol (owner from 1661 to 1677) and Thomas Osborne, Earl of Danby and Lord Treasurer (from 1677 to 1712).

38. John Evelyn (1620-1706).

The expert who advised both of them on the layout of their garden was the famous diarist, John Evelyn. Author of books on trees and gardens, he has been described as 'the dominant figure in gardening in England during the later seventeenth century'. After his travels in France during the Civil War, he had become a strong advocate of French fashions – 'grottos, fountains, rocks, aviaries, groves, statues, without which,' he claimed, 'the best garden is very defective'. He was also ready to give advice on very practical matters, like how to deal with 'catts' in the garden – 'to be hindered from scraping and basking by laying brambles and holly bushes in the beds'.

He paid at least three visits to Wimbledon in the early 1660s and two more in the late 1670s. His first sight of the garden on a February day in 1662 was not very promising: 'It is a delicious place for prospect and the thickets, but the soil cold and weeping clay'. Still, he returned four months later during the summer with a plan 'to contrive it after the modern'. The new layout had been made in consultation with the Earl of Bristol's head gardener, John Turner, who impressed him so much that he singled him out for special praise in his book *Sylva*. The details of this fourth change to the garden in less than eighty years are unknown. The Winstanley drawings made in 1678 are primarily of the house, while the final plan drawn about 1720 suggests changes on the plateau to the maze and wilderness. Some might have been made in the year Winstanley drew the house, but all Evelyn records of his visit to Danby in February 1678 is that he 'surveyed his gardens and alterations'.

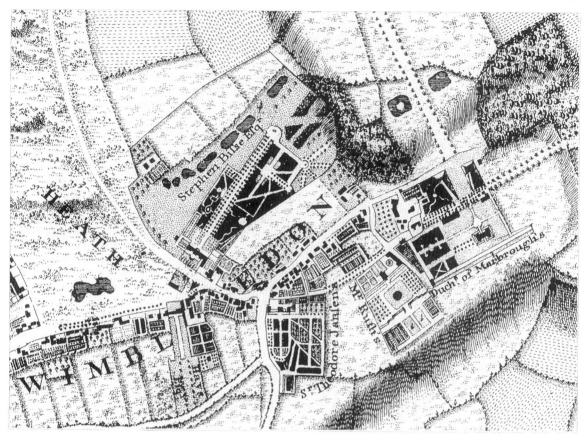

39. Part of a map of Wimbledon, published in 1746 by John Rocque. It shows the High Street in the centre with four of the great gardens to the east: the Duchess of Marlborough's around her manor house; that of Stephen Bisse MP in the grounds of Wimbledon House Parkside; Mr Rush's around Belvedere House; and Sir Theodore Janssen's opposite the Ridgway (in the 1790s added to the Belvedere gardens by Sir Beaumaris Rush).

For the next fifty years the gardens seem to have been left in peace. Then in the early 1730s the new Lord of the Manor, Sarah Duchess of Marlborough, decided to build a large mansion on top of the plateau, right over the site of the old maze. She employed Charles Bridgeman, gardener to King George II and supposed inventor of the ha-ha, to lay out a new formal garden south of the church. It replaced the Wilderness and was linked to an avenue of trees extending towards the Wandle. At the same time she had the orange and terrace gardens swept away.

In the 1760s, the rest of the formal gardens, including Bridgeman's, vanished at the hands of Lancelot 'Capability' Brown. His open park-like grounds reaching right up to the house transformed Wimbledon Park for Earl Spencer. But flowers were banished to the distant Kitchen Garden or Nursery at the bottom of Wimbledon Hill. Significantly the only allusion to this substitute for a garden among the Spencer family letters is from Sarah, daughter of the second Earl, who objected to going for long walks in the park with her mother. Instead, she far preferred a gentle stroll to the Nursery, 'full of lovely flowers, above all roses and violets'.

WIMBLEDON HOUSE, PARKSIDE

By this time the leading garden in Wimbledon was no longer that of the manor house, but one at Wimbledon House, Parkside. The mansion, built in the reign of Queen Anne, was unremarkable, but its hundred acre grounds (probably once part of the manor park) were said to command 'magnificent panoramic views' towards London. On a map of 1746 the garden is dominated by a long tree-lined avenue from the house leading to a

40. Benjamin Bond-Hopkins (1745-94), painted by Francis Wheatley.

semi-circular viewing point, as well as by a line of seven small ornamental lakes, probably once fish-ponds. The head gardener, John Martin, a Portuguese, looked after it for forty years 'with industry and success'. When he died in 1760, his employer, Sir Henry Bankes, had a special tombstone put up in the churchyard, 'as a lasting testimony of his great regard in so good a servant, a careful husband, a tender father and an honest man'.

All his careful work, however, was swept away in the 1770s by a new owner, Benjamin Bond-Hopkins. He wanted to model the grounds on Painshill Park, Cobham, which he had recently bought. So he employed Bushell, the designer of Painshill gardens, to lay out a series of large lakes with a 'cascade' (or waterfall) between the first two, a 'grotto' encrusted with shells and a 'wilderness' devoted to wildfowl. The grounds were

further improved after the end of the Napoleonic Wars by Mrs Marryat, a keen gardener and one of the first ladies to be elected a Fellow of the (Royal) Horticultural Society. She devoted much time and money to her hobby, introduced new plants (like rhododendrons and magnolias), as well as rare trees, and made her garden one of the finest near London. Like Sir Henry Bankes, she was grateful to her head gardener, William Redding, and when he died in 1853 after working in the garden for forty-six years, put up a tombstone in his honour.

The final owner of Wimbledon House, Sir Henry Peek MP, continued Mrs Marryat's work. He spent a great deal of money improving the grounds, above all building the most extensive range of greenhouses in the London area. In one of them he grew the heaviest bunch of bananas exhibited in Victorian England. He also kept a strange

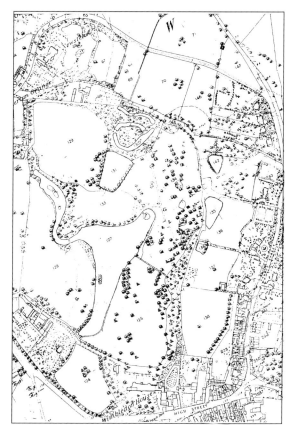

41. A map of the grounds of Wimbledon House Parkside in 1865, with the lakes designed by Bushell for Bond-Hopkins in the 1770s. Most are now drained.

assortment of animals, including Indian buffaloes, emus, Iceland sheep and ponies, as well as birds like parrots and New Guinea pigeons. On his death in 1898 his son sold the estate for development, but many of the fine trees survive in the gardens of the new houses.

EAGLE HOUSE GARDEN

Other Wimbledon mansions had fine grounds. Prospect Place, Copse Hill, was notable for its gardens, laid out by Humphry Repton in the early nineteenth century, as was Cannizaro under the Wilsons in the 1920s and '30s. But perhaps the most interesting of all was a seventeenth-century garden, recently discovered behind Eagle House in the High Street. Described in a Survey of 1617 as ' a fair new house' with a garden and orchard, the building was the home of Robert Bell, a London merchant (and one of the founders of the East India Company) whose family had lived in Wimbledon for the past hundred years. He was cer-

tainly very knowledgeable about gardens, having helped the Earl of Salisbury's gardener at Hatfield House, and perhaps also the Earl's half-brother with his garden at Wimbledon manor house. Such a man would undoubtedly want a good garden for himself.

In 1991 archaeologists from the Museum of London, led by Geoff Potter, were given permission to carry out an excavation of the garden before its development for houses. By careful digging, they discovered about a foot beneath the present surface the outline of an early seventeenth century formal garden, once enclosed by a brick wall and with a raised terrace at the opposite end to the house. It was rectangular and crossed by gravel and sand paths, probably lined with box hedges. Behind these were clay-lined bedding pits in which flowers once grew. No clue remained as to what these flowers might have been, but they probably included lilies, pansies, roses and even tulips which were just becoming popular. There was, however, no sign of one normal feature of a formal garden, a fountain.

42. David Thomson (1816-1905), a quiet unassuming Scotsman who ran a large Nursery at the bottom of Wimbledon Hill from 1852 until his death. As a leading landscape gardener there were few large new gardens in the area in which he did not have a hand.

43. *Wimbledon House Parkside in May 1894 during a display by the Fire Brigade.*

44. A typical gardneer in late Victorian Wimbledon, James Read, who worked at the Old Rectory.

The garden was maintained and probably improved under Bell's successors at Eagle House, the Bettensons (owners from 1647 to 1695). But under the Ivatts who held the estate for the first half of the eighteenth century, the formal garden seems to have been grassed over, thus sealing it in for future discovery. When the house became a school in 1789, it was probably used as a playground and only became a garden again in 1885 when Sir Thomas Jackson saved the house from demolition and restored it as a home. His fine paintings of the garden, ablaze with colourful flowers, is more to modern taste than the rather drab appearance of the previous formal garden.

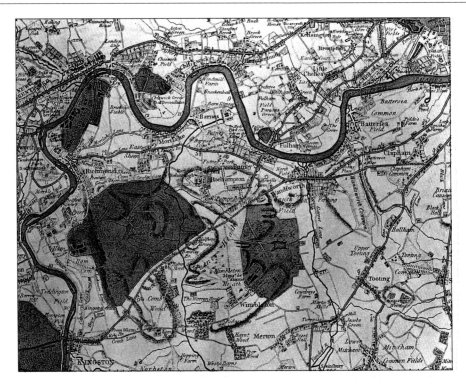

45. *A section of William Faden's map, the 'Country Twenty-Five Miles round London'
(1788), showing the roads used by the travellers, rich and poor, who came to Wimbledon
during the reign of George III. Those shaded are turnpike roads which were far better
maintained than those in the village.*

The Village, its Vestry and the Poor

A SMALL VILLAGE

The description of Eagle House as 'fair' and 'new' comes in a Survey made for the lord of the manor in 1617. This document, beautifully written on parchment, was compiled by Ralph Treswell, a London surveyor, with the help of four leading villagers. The Survey is invaluable because it provides the first full description of the village and its fields, though sadly it is not accompanied by a map.

The village (or 'Wimbletonn Towne') in the reign of James I was concentrated along just two roads – 'Towne Street' (our High Street) and 'Church Way' (Church Road). It consisted of forty-five 'tenements', mostly small cottages made of wattle and daub on a framework of wood, with a large hall, parlour and kitchen downstairs and three

bedrooms above. Behind was a 'backside' – a yard with a barn for corn and hay, and a stable for animals, along with a small garden and orchard. Only two houses were of any size: Robert Bell's home which dominated the High Street, and the twelve room mansion of the Walter family (the largest landowners apart from the Cecils) which equally dominated the road to the church. The village also had two inns: the small Sign of the White Hart in Church Way and the main hostelry, the Sign of My Lord's Arms, on the site of the present Dog and Fox.

The number of people in this tiny village can have been little more than 200, the same as a century earlier. Yet there were signs of growth. According to the Survey, six of the cottages had been 'newly built', while Manor Court records mention six villagers fined for 'erecting' cottages without four acres of land to go with them, to ensure they did not become refuges for poor families who would then be a burden on the rates.

Such a reaction reveals the big differences in wealth and outlook among the local people. At the top there were a few rich gentry, of whom the most notable was Sir William Walter. His grand-father had settled in the village in the 1550s and on his death in 1587 had been commemorated by a large monument, still on the north wall of St Mary's chancel. Sir William himself had been educated at Cambridge and the Inner Temple, and owned two things probably unique in Wimbledon at the time – a fine library and 'my coach and four horses'. To judge from his will, made just before his death in 1633, however, his wealth had not made him happy. He could not get on with his mother, his wife, or one of his daughters. So he left his most valuable possessions, including the library and coach, to 'my loving and obedient daughter, Katherine'.

Next in the social pyramid were the yeomen farmers, men like William Steadman who had moved to the village from Putney in 1597. He owned a large cottage in the High Street, farmed eighty acres and lived in considerable comfort, waited on by a 'made' servant, sleeping in a four-poster bed with a feather mattress and using napkins and 'table cloathes' at meals. Yet in his house there was no trace of a wash-basin and for a lavatory he and his family would have had to use a 'house of office' down the garden.

No shopkeepers are mentioned in the Survey, though other documents refer to a baker and a tailor. The first definite shop in the High Street seems to have been a butcher's, run by Phanuel Maybank who came from Kingston during the Civil War. There was, however, plenty of work for one important craftsman, the blacksmith. The village smithy was at 'Long's Corner', where the High Street joins Southside (its site is now the vet's). It was run by John Linton, who shod the villagers' horses, repaired their ploughs and carts, and made their farm implements, vital tasks if the fields were to be sown and harvested.

Equally important, though never regarded as such at the time, were the great majority of the villagers, the 'husbandmen' and labourers. Both had to work long hours for others and never found life easy or comfortable. Their tiny cottages would not have been draught-proof. Their food was poor. Their average wage, when work was available, was a shilling a day. Their expectation of a long life was never great. 'Their lives', one historian has written, 'were rich in nothing but hungry children'. A typical 'husbandman' is Richard Atkins who looked after Shepherd's Hatch Gate, one of the gates set up near the Common to prevent grazing animals from straying. It was situated about where the Crooked Billet pub is today and provided him with a tiny two-roomed cottage, 'an old shed and a backside'. Nothing else is known about him except that he farmed a

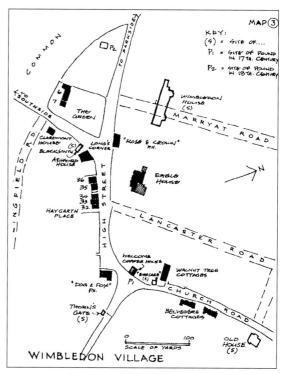

46. *A map of Wimbledon Village, drawn by John Wallace.*

small field off the Ridgway.

That plot of land (about where Christ Church is today) was at the far western corner of what had till recently been a large open field, extending as far as Wimbledon Hill on the east and Kingston Road to the south. Around 1613 Thomas Cecil and the other chief landowners had agreed to exchange their old scattered strips so as to form compact fields which they then enclosed with trees and hedges. The whole appearance of the land on and below the hill was thus transformed, as was the use of the fields. Along the Ridgway they were now kept as meadows on which cattle were grazed, while those on either side of 'Warpell Way' (our Worple Road) were mainly for growing corn. These fields were still there in 1865 and their lines often survive in modern property boundaries.

During the reign of George III another surveyor (whose name is nowhere recorded) made a 'Sketch of the Town of Wimbledon' for the then lord of the manor, the First Earl Spencer. Unlike Treswell, he produced a plan of the village, a very stylised one like a modern underground map. On it he recorded every building with the name of the occupant and in a key at the side he listed most of their jobs. Not all the information is accurate, but as a record of the village in 1776 the plan, like the earlier Survey, is quite invaluable.

In the intervening 160 years Wimbledon had clearly grown. The 45 tenements of 1617 had now increased to 145, with twenty extra to be added for others along the Ridgway and by the Wandle, neither of which were on the plan. The population had also grown: from around 200 in 1617 (via about 600 in 1700) to approximately 1000 in 1776. The extra inhabitants were virtually all immigrants, often from nearby villages like Putney, many drawn by the prospect of work in one of the big mansions, built recently round the Common. Significantly the names of families now living in the village were virtually all different from those listed in the parish register only fifty years earlier.

SHOPKEEPERS AND CRAFTSMEN

Among them were the shopkeepers who flourished in the newly-built brick shops (some of which still survive on the western side of the High Street opposite Eagle House). They included William Everett, the baker, who had recently arrived from Somerset; William Bodicote, the butcher, who had lived in the village since the 1740s and ran a dairy and slaughterhouse behind his shop; and John Edwards, the tailor, whose family had also been in the High Street for over thirty years. Round the corner in Church Lane there were also two grocers and two barbers.

Even more important than these shopkeepers were the craftsmen – carpenters, blacksmiths, 'bricklayers' (in fact builders), and wheelwrights, as well as a glazier and plumber, a harness-maker, a shoemaker and a sawyer. They were kept constantly at work – on repairs in the village, at the great mansions round the Common and at the Spencer manor house and park. Among them the most successful was one of the 'bricklayers', William Jennings, who lived in the High Street directly opposite Eagle House. His father had come from Bletchingley in Surrey in 1717 to marry a local girl. Within ten years he had taken on another 'bricklayer', was training an apprentice and was employing a boy and several labourers. William himself (one of seven children, three of whom died shortly after birth) became Vestry Clerk and succeeded his father as a builder, putting up cottages in the Crooked Billet and along Camp Road, which he then leased to local labourers. He also found time to run a small farm with a barn in Church Lane. After his death in 1784, his family continued to flourish in Wimbledon until well into the nineteenth century.

Along with shopkeepers and craftsmen, farmers were a significant influence in the village. Only one, John Paterson, lived near the High Street – in an old farmhouse that had once been the grange of the Archbishops of Canterbury. He was bailiff to Earl Spencer and managed his large farm in the park. His son, Benjamin, was to make a name for himself as 'a very scientific farmer' and to follow his father as the Earl's bailiff. Another successful farming dynasty were the Watneys. The founder, Daniel, came to Wimbledon from Hampton in 1730 on marrying a local girl and settled in a cottage in the Crooked Billet. He leased fields on either side of Worple Way and there grazed cattle, grew corn and even raised hops. His three sons all did well: William ran a brewery in the Crooked Billet; Thomas managed Warren Farm near Beverley Brook in the 1780s and '90s; John, the youngest, took over the father's land when he died in 1780 and on its growing profits built a fine house on Southside (now part of King's College Junior School).

RELIEF OF THE POOR

It was these village 'aristocrats' who virtually controlled local affairs through the Vestry. Before the Reformation meetings in the parish vestry had simply been concerned with the repair of the church. Under Queen Elizabeth, however, the vestry was given much wider responsibilities – for the repair of the highways and the relief of the poor – and far greater powers – to levy rates, to appoint local officials and make by-laws for the village, supervised only by the local Justices of the Peace. The Wimbledon Vestry was 'open', which meant that everyone who paid the rates could attend. In fact only about ten leading villagers (men like John Edwards, William Jennings and

47. 'The Bird Cage', a temporary lock-up for criminals at the top of Church Road, just before it was demolished about 1896. In the background is The Dog and Fox.

Daniel Watney) came regularly. They met on average about once a month in the church after Sunday morning service and promptly adjourned to the local inn. There under the chairmanship of the Vicar or the senior Churchwarden they discussed local affairs.

Their decisions, recorded in the Vestry Minutes (which have only survived from 1743), rarely sound exciting, as only occasionally is there any hint of their debates. Nonetheless, they seem to have given the village reasonably effective and conscientious government. They ensured law and order, and in times of crisis, as during the Napoleonic Wars, they provided leadership.

Their major problem was the relief of the poor. In the 1770s most villagers seem to have been 'in employ' and better off than their parents a generation earlier, an era plagued by smallpox, typhus and malaria. But there were now more 'impotent poor' – orphans, the chronically sick and the aged – who needed regular help. In addition, many families lived on the edge of poverty, especially during the winter when work was scarce.

The members of the Vestry, especially the two Overseers of the Poor, helped these unfortunate people. To the 'casual poor' who were temporarily 'out of employ', they gave small sums of money until they could find work. For the 'impotent' they at first provided small weekly pensions, as well as gifts of clothes and free medical treatment by the local apothecary. But in 1752 as the poor rate continued to rise, they ended 'outdoor relief' and set up a Workhouse in Camp Road. Its regime was very strict but it provided the destitute with three basic meals a day and a roof over their heads. On the other hand poor 'strangers' who tried to settle in the village were returned to their birthplace to stop them becoming a burden on the rates.

Yet despite all their efforts, as the population continued to rise, so did the poor rate. In the 1760s when there were about 800 people in the village, the Vestry had to raise about £250 a year for the poor. By 1800 with the population having doubled (1591 at the first official census in 1801), the rate had gone up over five times to £1300 – and it continued to rise until it reached just over £3000 a year in the early 1820s. The serious nature of the problem was partly the result of the Napoleonic Wars and their aftermath which disrupted trade, partly the effect of a long series of disastrous harvests since the 1790s which meant that bread and potatoes, the staple diet of the poor, became too costly for poor families. By 1811, 121 out of 291 householders had 'p' (too poor to pay) against their names in the Rate Books. To help them, wealthier villagers raised a 'subscription' to enable them to buy 'bread and potatoes at reduced

prices'. Even so, not long after the end of the French War, the Vestry Minutes recorded that 'for want of employment the labouring poor are now in the greatest distress and are daily increasing to an alarming degree'.

Treatment of the poor became a burning local issue. An increasing number of villagers began defaulting on payment of their rates and even wealthy landowners claimed that their assessments were too high. As a result there was a growing demand for a new system to calculate the rates. In 1826, along with Merton and Tooting, the Wimbledon Vestry promoted a bill in Parliament to make the owners of small cottages pay the rates rather than the poor occupiers. Their action led to a bitter controversy and did nothing to cut the large sums needed for poor relief. Only after the passing of a general Poor Law in 1834 were the rates dramatically cut, but only at the expense of the destitute poor. Their lives became infinitely worse in the new Poor Law Workhouses or 'Bastilles' (like the one at Kingston, now part of Kingston Hospital).

48. Part of a page of the Church Rate Book for 1822-23. The entries for Westside show that next to large mansions like Cannizaro ('Comte Sant Antonio', later Duke of Cannizzaro), Stamford House ('Mrs Ruddock') and The Keir ('Christopher MacEvoy Esq.') were small cottages whose occupiers (like 'Widow Beadle' of West Place) were too poor to pay anything.

49. *The earliest known photograph of the High Street, taken in about 1875. On the left is The Rose and Crown with its stables just beyond, and the rebuilt Dog and Fox in the background. On the right are the shops, already about a hundred years old. In the middle of the road is one of the original London omnibuses, setting off from its terminus at The Rose and Crown.*

50. *The High Street in the early 1920s, showing little sign of change except for the more modern buses and a few cars. Eagle House lies behind the railings on the left.*

Going to School

HUNGRY AND SICK CHILDREN

The ever-growing poor rate was certainly an unpleasant problem for members of the Vestry and the villagers who had to pay, but those who needed the help were infinitely worse off. Giving evidence to a House of Lords Committee on the Wimbledon Poor Law Bill in 1828, William Croft, a local builder who owned 28 cottages, revealed that the majority of his tenants were 'a great deal in arrears with the rent. They have five, six or seven children to support on just fifteen or sixteen shillings a week. They are in a state of starvation'.

Many of these children probably never grew up. In the 1790s when the Parish Register for once gave the ages of those buried in the churchyard, a quarter were 'infants' under a year old, and many older children also died every year, especially in August and September. Even wealthy families were not spared. Three sons of Earl Gower who lived at Wimbledon House on Parkside died within a few years of each other, while Earl Spencer's pretty younger daughter, Lady Georgiana Quin, died giving birth to a baby daughter Mary, who soon followed her mother to the grave. Still, it was the poor who suffered most the tragedy of family deaths. In 1821, for instance, the Penners, poor labourers who lived in a tiny cottage in Camp Road, received the terrible news that two of their sons, aged thirteen and nine, had just been killed. They had gone on the Common with two friends and there 'while employed in a gravel pit which had been left improperly excavated, were smothered by the sudden fall of earth above them'.

The children that did grow up had to survive that scourge of Georgian England, smallpox. In the early 1800s there were three serious outbreaks in the village. In one the Vestry was alerted to the danger by a Mrs Lee whose 'family were labouring under the smallpox and whooping cough'. So they allowed 'Mr Sanford, apothecary' to inoculate all poor children at parish expense. Just over two hundred were treated by this revolutionary cure, recently popularised by Edward Jenner. It seems to have brought the outbreak under control, only for it to return a few years later. This time, however, only about fifty children needed treatment.

Clearly many Georgian children had a hard life. Their staple diet was bread and cheese. Their clothes were poor. They had few toys – some marbles, a hoop or a skipping rope. Yet according to Dr Pamela Horn, most enjoyed a relatively happy childhood, 'secure in the love of their own

51. Ashford House in the High Street, the home of the apothecary, John Sanford and his large family. Built in the 1770s, it is shown here in 1908 just before the ground floor was converted into shops (which are still there today). The building on the right is part of the smithy.

family' and with the Common an ideal playground. They had to make their own amusements, not all of them very kind. One game, according to 'old folks' remembering their childhood in the 1830s, was 'to tie up a tempting bundle of sticks and fasten it to a long cord, then creep behind a hedge in the dark, and as an old lady came along and stooped to pick up the tempting prize, to jerk it quickly away and run off in the darkness with derisive laughter'.

A CHARITY SCHOOL

The first person to give practical help to such children was Lady Dorothy Cecil, the unmarried daughter of Edward Cecil, Viscount Wimbledon. In her will made in 1652 she left money to found a charity which would provide local boys and girls with apprenticeships outside Wimbledon. Though for a time the money was misappropriated by the trustees, the charity helped (and still helps) innumerable children to start a new life. One boy was sent to Battersea to learn market gardening; another went to Bermondsey to become a butcher, while a girl was taken on by a seamstress in London. Some village shopkeepers seem to have relied on the Cecil Charity to train their children. James Eades, a grocer in the High Street, who had himself come from Lambeth, had four of five sons apprenticed outside the village. Perhaps in return, local shopkeepers and craftsmen, like John Edwards the tailor and William Jennings the builder, trained apprentices themselves.

As a result, all leading Vestrymen and village officials could read, write and calculate by the 1750s (though their handwriting like that of 'Danel' Watney often left a lot to be desired). The last to

52. The 'Free' or 'Charity' School in Camp Road, photographed just before the First World War when it was known as the Old Central.

make 'his mark' on the Vestry Minutes was Francis Trevor, a poor man who had the distinction of being Wimbledon's first recorded centenarian, dying in 1778 aged 103. His inability to read or write was typical of the vast majority of poor villagers. In the 1750s members of the Vestry became very worried at 'the daily appearance of numerous poor children in the parish, destitute of the means of acquiring an orderly education'. They decided the only solution was to found their own Charity School.

So in 1757 they had a distinctive octagonal building put up as a schoolhouse on land Earl Spencer allowed them to take from the Common next to the Workhouse. Unfortunately they did not endow it with sufficient money and the master, Robert Johnson, was left unpaid. Sixteen years later they had to make a fresh start. They secured enough subscriptions from the wealthier villagers to set up 'the Wimbledon Free School', had the building repaired and provided a house for the new master, Joseph Andrews from Bermondsey, and his wife Sarah, who looked after the girls. Only children 'with some degree of instruction' were admitted and the curriculum was limited to 'the rudiments of reading and writing, so that they may be able to read the Bible or any other religious book, and to understand any direction in writing,

53. Countess Georgiana (1737-1814), wife of the 1st Earl Spencer. She took a personal interest in the school.

whereby it is hoped that they may be more likely to become good Christians and useful members of the community – but by no means be put above handicraft labour'.

The school had inevitable teething troubles. Absenteeism, abusive parents, children 'sent to school with the itch upon them and in a dirty and nasty condition', fathers needing their boys to help at harvest time and other children who 'neglect to come to church on Sundays', all disturbed the Vicar who chaired the committee controlling the school. But under the capable and hard-working master who insisted on firm discipline, the previously untapped abilities of some of his pupils were awakened. Helped by prizes of 'handsomely bound Bibles' for those who showed 'diligence and good progress' in reading and writing, they began to take pride in their work, encouraged by parents who were delighted to see them presented with their prizes in church at the end of Sunday morning service. Lists of the winners show that they often came from the same families, like those of John Edwards the tailor and William Everett the baker (whose daughter's Bible is now in the Wimbledon Society Museum).

The boys and girls stayed at school until they were about eleven or twelve. Some keen scholars wanted to stay on and had sadly to be told that they 'had received their education' and must leave. Most, however, needed help to get a job. In 1778 the Committee complained that the pupils after leaving 'generally lay unemployed for some time and fall into habits of idleness'. So they copied the Cecil Charity and started their own apprenticeship scheme. One of the first boys to benefit, John Blincowe, was taken on by John Watney, 'baker and farmer'.

PRIVATE SCHOOLS

The Wimbledon Free School clearly fulfilled a local need. The first two private schools, on the other hand, were meant for boarders from outside, including foreigners. Only one Wimbledon boy is known to have attended either school, the son of John Castle, the Parish Clerk, and his father got into trouble over late payment of the fees. For many years the sons of wealthy residents had been sent away to public schools, like the Walters in Tudor times to Westminster and the Spencers later to Harrow. Middle-class boys, like Robert Knox, son of a sea-captain in the 1640s, had been 'chiefly brought up under the education of my mother', especially through reading the Bible; later he had been sent to a small boarding school at Roehampton. There he had formed the simple, direct style that made his one book, *An Historical*

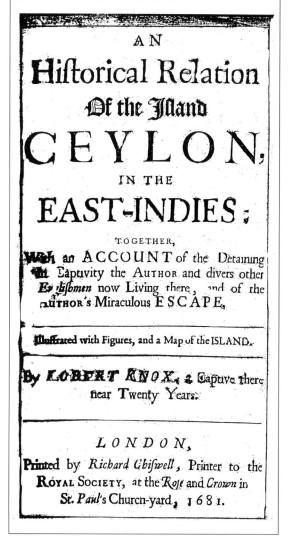

54. The title page of Robert Knox's book on Ceylon. Published in 1681, it interested many readers, including Charles II, and has been described as 'Wimbledon's first best-seller'.

Relation of the Island of Ceylon into a best-seller. So there may not have been much of a demand for fee-paying education in the village.

The Revd Thomas Lancaster, who set up the first private school in Wimbledon in 1790, seems to have chosen the village quite independently of any local need. He heard that one of its finest older buildings, Eagle House on the High Street with its gardens and seventeen acres of land, had just come on the market for £2,300. He calculated that 'an Academy for young noblemen and gentlemen'

55. *Eagle House School, described as 'An Ancient Mansion' and drawn in 1827 by John Buckler.*

in such a 'large and commodious house' and in a 'situation most healthful' would impress wealthy parents. He also hoped he would meet with no competition. A few years earlier he had started a school just across the Thames at Parsons Green, but had found pupils hard to attract. He was sure that it would be different in Wimbledon.

He was right. The school was soon regarded as one of the best near London. Four resident teachers provided a wide curriculum, while part-timers came from London for those who wanted to learn drawing, dancing, fencing and music. The sixty boys between six and sixteen were looked after by the Matron, Lancaster's daughter, and the food seems to have been adequate. But the method of teaching – everything to be learnt by heart and tested every Saturday – antagonised at least one pupil, the future German philosopher, Arthur Schopenhauer. Sent to school for twelve weeks while his parents went on a tour of the British Isles, he found Lancaster's methods very different from the liberal regime of his school in Hamburg. He was bored, did not get on with the English boys and came to regard the place as a prison.

His reaction to Wimbledon might have been different had his Headmaster been the Revd Samuel Catlow, a Nonconformist minister. In 1811 Catlow started a 'Literary and Commercial Seminary' at South Hayes (now part of King's College School) on Southside. Like Lancaster, he took boys from six to sixteen and insisted they worked hard. But

he placed far more emphasis on sport, on food chosen by 'the inclination of the pupil' and on lessons which aroused the boys' interest and did not demand simply parrot knowledge. Sadly the school only lasted a few years in the strongly Anglican atmosphere of Wimbledon. Lancaster's, on the other hand, continued to flourish. After he retired to his parish of Merton in 1811, a succession of headmasters took over; the last, the Revd John Brackenbury, was so successful that in 1860 he was able to move to a larger, purpose-built school on Edge Hill.

The home life of the pupils at these schools is nowhere recorded. The only children whose letters have survived are those of the Spencer family at the manor house. George, the future Second Earl, wrote to his mother that he missed her, but was playing with his toy soldiers – 'a whole troop of light horse made of lead', with which he 'besieged card cities'. When he went to Harrow, he wrote regularly about playground games (prisoner's base, marbles, tops), studies (Latin, Greek and public speaking) and relations with the masters (surprisingly friendly, though there was a small mutiny against the Headmaster). He was also pleased to be allowed to have a small garden of his own, in which he planted ' a great many flowers I had from Wimbledon', and to keep a wonderful assortment of pets – a dog, cat, canary, jackdaw and four young blackbirds, 'which I keep in a garret away from the cat'. No wonder he seems to have enjoyed

56. *The Revd John Brackenbury (1816-95). An outstanding schoolmaster, he was appointed joint head of Nelson House School in the High Street in 1849. He proved so successful that eleven years later he moved to a new, much larger building in Edge Hill. There he prepared older boys for entry into the Royal Military Academies. He also acted as Chairman of the Local Board from 1871 to 1876.*

58. *The Revd Edward Huntingford (1820-1905), who gave Eagle House its name. In 1860 he took over the school there from Brackenbury, brought with him a stone eagle and fixed it onto the central gable where it has stayed ever since. His school prepared young boys for public schools and was so successful that in 1886 it moved to a larger building at Camberley, where the school still flourishes.*

57. *South Hayes, a mansion along Southside, which became a boarding school for boys in the 1820s. This picture of the garden front was taken in 1892, five years before King's College School moved there from the Strand.*

59. *A picture taken about 1907 of girls from the Study at Margin Lake (created in the 1770s in the grounds of Wimbledon House Parkside). The school had begun in 1893 at a converted shop in the High Street. Ten years later it moved to its present building in Peek Crescent.*

60. *Children leaving Queens Road County School about 1910. It had been opened eight years earlier for both boys and girls, and soon had well over a thousand pupils.*

61. Girls at the Old Central School with their choir master, Mr Bates, after winning several cups for singing at a Baths Hall music festival in the 1930s.

his years at school, though like all schoolboys towards the end of term he longed for the holidays to start.

His eldest daughter Sarah spent a lot of her childhood at Wimbledon, living in 'the Nursery', the old servants' quarters later used as the core of Henry Holland's manor house of 1801. She was educated by governesses and when only nine was able to write to her grandmother in French: 'At Christmas I was given a lot of nice things, above all a wax doll, the loveliest I have ever seen'. Later she told her: 'I am teaching Bob [a younger brother] to read English', but complained: 'Mr Bob makes such a noise that I can hardly write anything'. She was fourteen when the family moved into their new Wimbledon home and was thrilled to be given her own boudoir, 'furnished with all my prettiest books in a little bookcase, a little tiny sofa and two or three chairs and a table. You can't think how pretty it looks. I can hardly persuade myself to leave it and I settle and unsettle the chairs, books and tables all day long'.

The Spencer children were indeed fortunate, as Sarah herself recognised after being given four 'very well bound books' by her father as New Year presents. She remarked to her brother: 'Aren't we lucky to have such good parents!'

62. Sarah, daughter of the 2nd Earl Spencer, drawn by her mother showing off a pair of new shoes.

Two Georgian Parks

Soon after the Spencer family inherited the Marlborough manor house in 1744, John Rocque published a map of the *Country Ten Miles round London*. The Wimbledon section marks two large parks: the New or Manor Park (about 300 acres in extent, but soon considerably enlarged) and the Old Park or 'The Warren' (also covering about 300 acres).

Neither of these Georgian parks was by then fulfilling the purpose for which it had originally been created – as enclosures for deer and rabbits. Surrounded by 'the park pale', a stout wooden fence, they had been carved out of large areas of 'the waste' (perhaps once part of the Common) where deer could be reared and then hunted more easily than in the wild. Inside the pale there were also stewponds for fish and specially constructed warrens for 'coneys' or rabbits, whose meat, like venison, was considered a special delicacy and served at banquets. Such parks had started on royal estates in the Middle Ages, but by Tudor times they had become a status symbol for great noblemen and churchmen.

THE OLD PARK

The early history of the Old Park is uncertain. It was probably created by one of the medieval Archbishops of Canterbury. The first hint of its existence comes in 1328, at a time of unrest after the deposition of King Edward II, when 'evil-doers' were accused of felling the trees and hunting and killing the deer in the Archbishop's 'park and woods at Wimbledon'. This park is first given a position to the west of the Common in a Manor Court document of 1574 and in John Norden's map of Surrey drawn twenty years later. Its exact boundaries appear in the 1617 Survey of the manor. In modern terms they extended from Westside across to Beverley Brook and from Caesar's Camp to the region of Drax Avenue (right across the present Royal Wimbledon golf course). Within the park there was a lodge for the Park-keeper or Ranger. Referred to as 'the Half-Moon' because of its unusual shape, it was said to be situated 'within an old fort called the Benchberry Fort' (our Caesar's Camp), the highest point in the park so that the Ranger could keep an eye on all that was going on. There was also 'another house where the warrener lives' (our Warren Farm). His job

63. *A map of Wimbledon Park in 1765, showing its increased size and the chief changes made by 'Capability' Brown.*

was to look after 'the two warrens of coneys' and the fishponds (near Beverley Brook and commemorated today by Fishpond Wood).

In 1536 the Old Park was taken over from Archbishop Cranmer by King Henry VIII. A hundred years later it was used by Charles I when he was creating a New Park at Richmond. He was assured that the neighbouring Old Park was a secure enclosure in which to keep his precious roe deer while the Richmond wall was being built. Unfortunately it proved not to be the case. Some deer escaped and were killed by poachers 'in the woods adjoining'. A furious King wrote to one of his leading Councillors, the Marquess of Hamilton: 'We give straight charge to your servants that they suffer not any person of what degree soever to come into your woods with any gun, greyhound or engine to take or destroy the game'. His orders, however, seem to have had little effect.

Just before the Civil War, the park (now called Half-Moon Park) passed into private hands, the lodge was demolished and the deer disappeared for good. But the coney warrens were still in use in the early eighteenth century. In 1723 poachers waylaid and beat up two of the warreners, attacked their house and fired at an upstairs window from which a woman had shouted at them. Fortunately no one was hit, but the poachers escaped. Perhaps as a result of this escapade, combined with the building of Westside and Cannizaro houses on the edge of the Common, the warrens seem to have been abandoned and most of the Old Park turned into a farm (the rest became 'the pleasure grounds' of the two houses). The new fields surrounding Warren Farm were given expressive names like Bog Field, Newfoundland, Broom Field, Calves' Close, Hilly Field and Fox Field. They were looked after by many different farmers. The only famous names among them were Thomas Watney and his son Matthew who managed the farm between 1785 and 1812. Only one incident in its long history has been recorded. In his memories of life at Cannizaro in the 1860s, Canon Boustead recalled 'a beautiful bull' at the farm. It was 'docile to those it liked'. Unfortunately 'the bailiff was unable to control it. One evening the bull, infuriated by something, broke the chain, rushed at the bailiff and gored him to death. His shriek was so awful and so loud that it reached even to the village'. In 1907 the farm finally disappeared and the fields were transformed into the Royal Wimbledon golf course. Just over forty years later the other surviving part of the Old Park, the grounds of Cannizaro, became a public park.

THE NEW PARK

The early history of the New or Wimbledon Park is also uncertain. It is first mentioned by name in the Survey of 1617, when it extended from Durnsford Lane on the east to the Common on the west, and from 'the Vineyard' in the manor house garden in the south to 'Wansworth Common' on the north. But almost certainly it had been created thirty years earlier by Sir Thomas Cecil when he built his new 'prestige house', and it was here that he entertained Queen Elizabeth in the 1590s and King James I in 1616 with a hunt.

During the Civil War Sir Richard Wynn did his best to look after the park for the Queen. He hired watchmen and two bloodhounds to guard the deer from poachers, but by the time of the Parliamentary Survey in 1649 only ten of the animals were left. In the 1650s General John Lambert seems to have preferred hawking in the park with birds sent from Scotland by General Monk. Twenty years later the Earl of Danby restocked the park with French deer from Versailles, provided by the English Ambassador, and employed Charles Palmer as 'huntsman'. Whether he hunted with guests such as William of Orange or even the Tsar Peter the Great is not recorded. If so, they would have been among the final meets in the park. Once Sarah, Duchess of Marlborough, bought the manor in 1723, she took little interest in the park, complaining that 'the people hereabouts use me very ill; they destroy all my game and come into the very park and gardens to do so'.

When the Spencers inherited the manor in 1744, a new era opened for the park. Trustees for the young First Earl added to it a large area of Southfields, along with Ashen Grove Farm. Then in 1760, after the Earl himself had taken control, 'Capability' Brown was commissioned to make improvements. He so transformed the appearance of the park with a large lake, wide vistas through the woods and a new winding drive from the road to London that a journalist was moved to write: 'The ground about Lord Spencer's place at Wimbledon is perhaps as beautiful as anything near London. Nature has done much for it and Brown made of it much more'. The Earl was delighted, telling his son in 1777: 'Wimbledon is in the highest order of beauty with the most lovely verdure that can be seen', while the son, George, when only twelve had already decided that the park in summer was 'the prettiest place in the world'.

64. John, 1st Earl Spencer (1734-83).

Earl SPENCER.

The Spencers not only admired the park, but put it to very practical use. They held great garden parties, called 'breakfasts' so as to persuade guests not to overstay their welcome. They went boating and fishing on the lake, which they persisted in calling 'the pond'. They set up a menagerie near the main drive where they kept animals and birds. They enjoyed riding or going for long walks. Above all, the first two Earls, father and son, loved shooting in special 'coverts' for partridges, pheasants and hares, created just off Parkside (where Inner Park Road is today). To ensure that the birds were not disturbed, they employed game-keepers who ruthlessly enforced the game laws. In 1788, for example, when the pet dog of a neighbouring landowner happened to stray into the park, it was not merely shot, but had its throat 'cut from ear to ear'. The owner naturally sent a letter of protest, but the Earl was quite unrepentant.

As an 'improving landlord', he was just as concerned over his two hundred acre farm in the park. Originally managed from an old weatherboarded house near the church, the Earl moved

65. *George, 2nd Earl Spencer (1758-1834), in 1809.*

66. *Wimbledon Park in the early years of Queen Victoria's reign. This painting by an unknown artist shows the park from a drive, with the lake in the middle distance.*

its headquarters in 1809 to Ashen Grove farm-house on Durnsford Lane. This farm had been developed just before the Civil War and had been owned by the Spencers only since the 1750s. It was, however, right in the centre of their great block of fields, covering the eastern half of the park between the lake and the Wandle (where 'the Grid' of roads around Wimbledon Park station is today). Wheat, barley, oats, hay and turnips were grown in fields near the Wandle, while a large flock of sheep and 'a choice stock of dairy cows' (all with names like Myrtle) grazed in Ladder Stile Field and Vineyard Hill Field nearer the lake. Round the farm there were also a model dairy, a slaughter-house, hen, duck and goose 'houses', along with a pond.

The Earl's chief problem, however, was to find the right man to run the farm. After several failures, he finally asked Benjamin Paterson, the son of his father's old bailiff, to take over in 1809. Paterson had made his name running Cowdrey Farm, Wimbledon's oldest private farm, which had flourished since at least the late Middle Ages. It was situated to the south of Ashen Grove, with fields extending westwards above the road to Merton (our Broadway) as far as the bottom of Wimbledon Hill. He gained a reputation as 'a scientific farmer' by introducing here one of the new threshing-machines which separated corn from the stalk more efficiently than a flail. He soon transformed Wimbledon Park Farm. One year he produced a hay harvest which 'surprised everybody by its immense profusion', and continued to farm the land profitably, despite the slump in the price of wheat after the end of the war with France in 1815. His son took over when he retired and the farm was only given up when the District Line was driven through its fields in the 1880s and the surrounding roads (including Ashen Grove) laid out in the early 1900s.

By then Wimbledon Park itself had also nearly disappeared. Along with the farm and manor house, it had been sold in 1846 by the 4th Earl Spencer for £80,000. The purchaser, John Augustus Beaumont, was an insurance company director and property developer. In the 1850s he laid out roads in the northern half of the park and sold sizeable plots of land on which large Victorian mansions were built for wealthy men like John Murray, the publisher. By 1865 *The Times* could report that 'Wimbledon Park, which a few years ago could have been bought at £150 an acre, is now

67. *John Augustus Beaumont (1806-86). In the 1860s he lived with his family in Wimbledon Park House and used the lake for boating and fishing parties.*

worth £1000 an acre and is covered with stately villas'. Beaumont then decided to develop the southern half round the manor house. Here, however, few plots were sold until the District Railway was opened in 1889. Then roads and houses went up at such a rate that in 1913 it was proposed to drain the lake and build roads right across the surviving part of the park, then leased to sports clubs (especially the Wimbledon Park Golf Club). Just in time Wimbledon Council decided to step in and buy the last 150 acres round the lake from Beaumont's daughter, Lady Lane, for £66,500. The deeds were finally signed on 29 December 1915 and ten years later a public park was opened next to the lake. As with the Old Park, the New has been preserved as a mixture of golf course and municipal park.

Four Georgian Residents

70. *John Horne Tooke (1736-1812) who lived at Chester House, Westside, from 1792 until his death. He was a leading opponent of Pitt's government and in 1794 was accused of high treason. But he put up a brilliant defence and was found not guilty.*

68. *William Wilberforce (1759-1833) inherited Lauriston House, Southside in 1777 and often stayed there. In 1786 he moved to Clapham where he dedicated his life to the abolition of the slave trade.*

69. *William Pitt (1759-1806) never owned a house here but did stay with his friends Wilberforce at Lauriston House and William Grenville his cousin at Eagle House; above all with his closest confidant, Henry Dundas at Cannizaro.*

71. *A monument to James Perry (1756-1821) in the porch of St Mary's church. Perry was editor of The Morning Chronicle, an influential radical newspaper. In 1796 he took over the corn mill on the Wandle and lived with his large family at Wandlebank House nearby.*

Wimbledon in 1838

AMERICANS IN WIMBLEDON

Wimbledon Park may have been in danger of completely disappearing in 1913, yet 75 years earlier it had been the scene of a Grand Fête to celebrate the young Queen Victoria's coronation. Though still owned by Earl Spencer it had been leased to the Duke and Duchess of Somerset. They used the house and grounds as a summer retreat and in 1837 had already invited the Queen (shortly after her accession) to a garden party on the lawns. Victoria drove there from London with her uncle, the Duke of Sussex, and when they got near the house, local people unharnessed the horses and pulled her to the front porch.

At the Coronation Fête a year later one of the guests was Mrs Stevenson, wife of the United States Ambassador. In her memoirs she described the occasion as 'the affair of the season'. The Queen arrived at about six o'clock and 'promenaded the grounds where the company had assembled on rich carpets, with sofas and chairs'. Meanwhile Tyrolean minstrels, Russian dancers, Alpine singers and Highland pipers provided entertainment. Then the Duke and Duchess led the Queen into dinner in a 'very beautiful marquee, its roof supported by twelve columns, the interior lined with crimson stripes'. Four hundred and fifty guests sat down to a large meal, while a military band played light music. At the end of the dinner, 'the extremely pretty illuminations' were set off and 'the ball commenced in the tent'.

Mrs Stevenson chose this moment to 'make my escape'. She went to see a fellow American, Mrs Charlotte Marryat, now one of Wimbledon's leading personalities. A month earlier she had spent a week at the Marryat home, Wimbledon House Parkside, recovering from illness. She had been impressed with the house, 'one of the most beautiful villas in England', with its garden, 'quite a showplace', and with her hostess, 'now a widow, employing herself in good works'.

Mrs Marryat had been married to a wealthy businessman and Member of Parliament, but in 1824 he had suddenly collapsed and died. She had

72. A map of Wimbledon in 1865. It could almost be dated 1838 as little change has occurred since the railway arrived over 25 years earlier. New Wimbledon is beginning to rise along the Broadway and Hartfield Road, but most of the houses are still on the top of the hill.

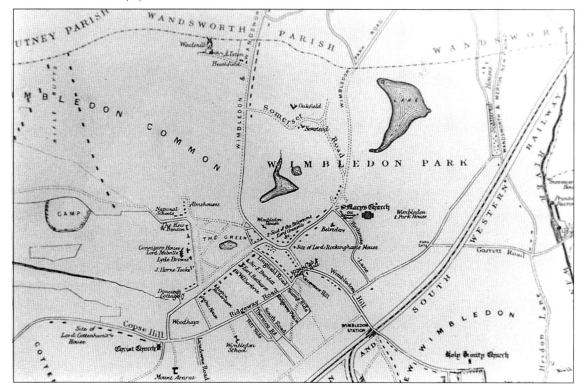

73. *Mrs Charlotte Marryat (1773-1854), a rich American from Boston. She lived at Wimbledon House Parkside from 1812 until her death and was said to have been 'as much thought of at Wimbledon as the Queen at Windsor'.*

since devoted herself to her large family (including Frederick, a captain in the Navy and famous novelist), to her garden where she introduced new plants including rhododendrons, and to 'good works'. A keen Evangelical, she presided at family prayers every evening, went on Sundays with other ladies to the gypsy encampment in Caesar's Camp to read them the Bible and held a fair in her grounds to raise money for new Almshouses to replace the old Workhouse in Camp Road.

SUPPRESSION OF WIMBLEDON FAIR

The Almshouses, so important if poor elderly people in the village were to escape the dreaded new Union Workhouse in Kingston, were opened in 1838 shortly before the Coronation Fête. But already Mrs Marryat was aiming at another 'moral improvement'. She strongly disapproved of the Fair held in the High Street every Easter Monday as it attracted, according to Earl Spencer, 'all sorts of London blackguards'. So, helped by the Curate at St Mary's, the Revd Mr Edelman, she lobbied the members of the Vestry and finally in 1840 secured its suppression on the grounds that 'its moral effect on the people was so bad'.

Only one member of the Vestry, Major-General Sir Henry Murray, was strong-minded enough to oppose her. Son of the Earl of Mansfield and a soldier who had distinguished himself leading a

74. *General Sir Henry Murray (1784-1860), son of the Earl of Mansfield. He is commemorated by Murray Road, laid out over the site of his house in 1905.*

cavalry charge at Waterloo, he lived at Wimbledon Lodge, a fine 'Greek revival' house on Southside. He argued strongly that the Fair was an old village custom, one of the few festivals 'which the labouring classes have the opportunity of enjoying'. His speeches had little effect, except to impress his fellow Vestrymen with his character. Two years later when he had to leave Wimbledon for a time to serve on the Staff in Ireland, they unanimously thanked him for his 'advice and urbanity', added that his 'politeness and kindness' had made him 'highly respected' and hoped he would soon return.

VILLAGE AFFAIRS

These members of the Vestry who ran local affairs included some of the leading villagers: James Courthope Peache, a timber merchant from Lambeth, who had recently bought (and named) Belvedere House; Adam Hogg, a colonel in the East India Company's Army, who lived in Holme Lodge, one of the two houses later united as Southside House; Thomas Mason, the leading

75. *The front of Wimbledon Lodge, Southside, about 1806. It had been designed by a young architect, Aaron Hurst, in the early 1790s for 'an eminent merchant', Gerard de Visme. On his death in 1797, it was inherited by his illegitimate daughter Emily, who married General Murray.*

76. *James Courthope Peache (1781-1858). A loyal Anglican, he played an important part as churchwarden in the rebuilding of St Mary's in the early 1840s.*

High Street grocer and local Postmaster; George Croft, a builder and timber merchant of West Place, who owned forty-two cottages; and Richard Blake, who had recently taken over Cowdrey Farm near the Wandle. In the late 1830s they were very concerned about the state of the Common – the dangerous condition of the gravel pits, obstructions in the horse rides and 'the decreasing salubrity of the air arising from the number of stagnant pools'. The two Colonels, Murray and Hogg, were deputed to see Earl Spencer, but with no practical result. At the same time the Vestrymen were also concerned at the 'very limited number of parishioners' who were able to 'join in the service of Almighty God' as St Mary's only had room for a congregation of about seven hundred. So they resolved to increase its capacity, first by trying to rearrange the sittings and when that failed by the more drastic method of pulling down the Georgian nave and commissioning Gilbert Scott and William Moffit to build a new one – a move strongly opposed by General Murray. The result, however, was an impressive Victorian church with a distinctive spire and large nave, which the Archbishop of Canterbury consecrated in 1843.

The chief concern of the Vestry in 1838, however, was law and order. After 'a dangerous attack' had been made 'upon a gentleman on Wimbledon Common', they appointed two special constables, David Penner and Thomas Dann, the miller. Dann was chosen as his Windmill overlooked a favourite spot for duels, 'a lawn-like land with a small stream running through it (the site of the later Queensmere). In August 1838, John Mirfin, a young linen-draper, was killed in a duel there with another young man, Francis Elliott, after their carriages had collided when driving to London (an early Victorian example of 'road rage'). Dann had not then been able to intervene, but two years later he arrived on the scene just after the Earl of Cardigan had shot his opponent, Captain Harvey Tuckett, in the chest. He arrested Cardigan and escorted him to Wandsworth police station, while his wife dressed Tuckett's wounds. Cardigan was tried by the House of Lords and acquitted. But his behaviour seems to have discredited duelling and so the Vestry had one less problem to give them concern, especially as they now had their first professional policeman, Sergeant Pinegar, who lived at 1, Brickfield Cottages on the Ridgway (now 1 Oldfield Road).

Two very different opinions of the village they tried to manage were given in contemporary reference books. Pigot's *New Commercial Directory* of 1834 described it as 'a beautiful and highly genteel village which is surrounded by the seats of the nobility and gentry'. Yet *The Railway Companion* of 1839, describing what could be seen on a journey from Nine Elms, dismissed it as a mere 'hamlet', though it had 'a number of elegant villas', while at its two inns there was 'abundant accommodation and entertainment'. Wimbledon may have been a hamlet in medieval times, but by 1838 it had become a sizeable village with over four hundred 'inhabited houses' and a population of around 2,500, a thousand more than at the start of the century. There were still plenty of poor families living just off the High Street, especially near the Dog and Fox, where Beehive Buildings, Mutton Alley and Carter's Alley consisted of rows of small cottages, built back-to-back, housing farm labourers, gardeners and laundresses. Yet in the High Street itself and in Church Lane there were plenty of small thriving shops, including four grocers, three bakers, dairymen, tailors and boot- and shoemakers, two butchers and 'fruiterers', a hairdresser (appropriately John Barber) and even the first fishmonger, William Frost. There was also real choice among the tradesmen: several builders, carpenters (who also acted as undertakers), plumbers and blacksmiths (one describing himself as a 'veterinary surgeon'), along with a rat-catcher and well-borer. Finally along with The Dog and Fox and The Rose and Crown, there were now four 'Beer Retailers' and two brewers. Yet if all these businesses suggest crowds regularly thronging the streets, a revealing story about the village stocks at the corner of Church Lane and the High Street shows how fairly deserted they often were. Old folk remembered seeing a man sitting in the stocks about the year Victoria became Queen, but added that there was 'no one to see him; there might not be more than half a dozen people passing that way in the whole day'.

CANNIZARO HOUSE

Among those who most certainly would not have passed that way, except on Sundays when going to church, were the nobility and gentry who lived in the 'elegant villas' round the Common. Notable among them were two individuals who have given their names to houses or districts of present-day Wimbledon: the Duchess of Cannizzaro and Charles Pepys, Earl of Cottenham. The Scottish Duchess and her Italian husband have been described as 'two most colourful characters'. They had married in 1814, she apparently because he was 'good-looking, intelligent and of high birth' (a Sicilian Count and later Duke), he mainly for her money – she was 'a beautiful heiress, totally uneducated, but full of humour'. Three years later they leased Warren House (the later Cannizaro) as a country retreat and there entertained many famous people, including Mrs Fitzherbert, the real wife of George IV, Countess Esterházy, wife of the Austrian Ambassador, and the great Duke of

77. Sophia Johnstone, Duchess of Cannizzaro (1788-1841).

78. The garden front of Cannizaro House about 1920. With its large verandah, it was the only part of the Queen Anne building to have been saved when the rest of the house was burnt down in 1900. The children with the dog are the daughter of Mr and Mrs Wilson, the owners, and her young friends. Behind them, the statue of Diana the Huntress has since been exiled to the far end of the park.

79. Charles Pepys, Earl of Cottenham (1781-1851) in his robes as Lord Chancellor.

Wellington. But in 1833 the rather incongruous marriage broke up. The Duke went off to Italy with a Mme Visconti and the Duchess consoled herself with her 'all-absorbing interest', music. She was a great patron of musicians, built up her own valuable music library, and fell in love with 'a strapping young Italian singer'. Then in 1841, as suddenly as they had erupted into the life of Westside, they disappeared. They both died within a few months of each other and when William Mason, acting as enumerator for the census that summer, called at the house he found only servants there. So on his form, with no owner to record, he gave the place a name – 'Cannazerro House'. The name somehow stuck in local directories, finishing in 1874 with the present spelling 'Cannizaro'.

THE COMING OF THE RAILWAY

Charles Pepys, Earl of Cottenham, gave his name not merely to a house, but to a road and a whole district in West Wimbledon. In 1831 he bought Prospect Place and its 250-acre estate between Copse Hill and Coombe Lane with grounds 'improved' by Humphry Repton thirty years earlier. He wanted it to be a real home where he, his wife and their fifteen children could have peace and quiet in beautiful surroundings. Though a successful barrister, an able judge and from 1836 to

1841 Queen Victoria's first Lord Chancellor, he cared little for society and, when his work at Westminster was finished for the day, drove straight home for 'his hour of peace and joy when he went up to the nursery to sing his little ones what he called Chinese songs'. Such a man would hardly welcome the appearance of noisy, dirty trains on his estate.

The idea of building one of the new railways to link London and Southampton had first been put forward in 1830, before the Earl had moved to Wimbledon. But the survey of a possible route, made by Francis Giles, a leading canal engineer, came just after his arrival and met with his total opposition as it ran right across the southern part of his estate. So Giles was forced to move the line south of Worple Lane into 'the lowlands' where the chief landowner, Caroline Phillips, the only legitimate child of Benjamin Bond-Hopkins, was ready to sell blocks of fields to the railway company. But the change meant the creation of a long, high embankment (using earth from the cutting at Surbiton) to keep the gradient level for the early trains, and the building of bridges and tunnels to preserve old rights of way.

The line was thus not ready to be opened (and then only as far as Woking) until May 1838. Heavy rain damaged the early embankment, local contractors were inefficient and Giles showed little drive. In 1837 he was replaced by Joseph Locke,

80. *Prospect Place in the 1840s. The house, built about 1750, had been added to by later owners. It was pulled down a few years after the Earl's death. New houses are now going up on its site.*

a pupil of George Stephenson, inventor of the Rocket. He promptly sacked all the contractors and gave the work to Thomas Brassey, who later made his name building railways all over the world. He transformed affairs and a year later was able to hold two trial runs from the terminus at Nine Elms near Vauxhall to Woking. The train went at the astonishing speed of thirty miles an hour and the journey was said to have been 'smooth and easy'. It was watched 'on every eminence along the line' (such as Wimbledon Hill), by 'admiring rustics who gathered in thousands to cheer the trains'. So on Monday 21 May when the line was opened to the public, people flocked to use it – except at Wimbledon.

The small new station, labelled 'Wimbledon and Merton' because it was half-way between the two villages, was right out in the country where it could only disturb the cows and a few farm workers. Round it were just three buildings. On the Merton side of the new iron bridge over the tracks was the home of the stationmaster, Ben Bradford along with a cottage where lived the railway policeman (who also acted as signalman and ticket collector). On the other side was The Mansel Arms, a new railway pub which acted as a ticket office and where passengers had to go down a steep flight of stairs to reach the small platform to the west of the bridge. There they might have to wait two to three hours – unless they had seen one of the tiny time-tables – as there were just five trains a day each way.

It is therefore hardly surprising that at first most Wimbledonians were not very eager to use the railway. As late as 1845 the average number of passengers boarding one of the trains at the station was about a hundred a day. One of those who did travel up to London shortly after the line was opened was Edward Rayne, the owner of West Barnes Farm, who had himself helped to bring gravel and rails for the track. He was obviously pleased with the speed of the journey, recording in his diary: 'I went and returned from town by the railway and was home again by noon'.

Nonetheless, even after the railway opened, four of the old short-stage coaches continued to ply every day between the village and London. They cost about double the first-class train fare to Nine Elms, but took passengers all the way to the City. In Church Lane there were also two 'flys', open-front cabs which could be hired for journeys from door to door. The post, however, was still fairly primitive. There was only one 'letter carrier', John Culverwell, who lived in Almshouse Lane (our Camp Road). He had to collect the letters from Thomas Mason, 'Letter Receiver' (as well as grocer) at the top of the High Street. He then had to walk to Putney with them, collect the letters for Wimbledon at the Post Office there and on his return to the village deliver them to addresses he had to remember from the names of the householders as there were no street numbers.

Wimbledon in 1838 was on the verge of major changes with a large railway embankment that effectively cut the parish in two and was to have profound social consequences.

'New Wimbledon': The rise of a railway suburb

THE FIRST COMMUTERS

The major changes first began to appear in the 1860s. By then Wimbledon had become an important railway junction after the opening of four extra lines: in 1855 to West Croydon (linking there with the Brighton line), then four years later to Epsom via the future Raynes Park Station (opened in 1871), next in 1868 to Tooting via 'Haydons Lane' (and on to London Bridge) and finally the following year to Kingston via New Malden. The extra lines meant a new layout at the station with platforms on the north of the bridge for the Croydon and Kingston services; followed in 1884 by the building of a new booking office there for the London and South-Western trains and then five years later by an extra station for the new District Line from Putney Bridge.

One man who moved to Wimbledon from Mitcham in 1864 to use the improved railway service

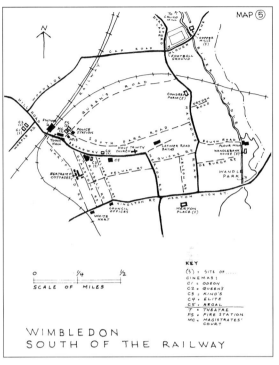

82. A map of New Wimbledon, drawn by John Wallace.

81. The view from The Prince of Wales public house in 1880, with the narrow iron bridge over the railway, the platforms on both sides of the bridge, the station forecourt with piles of coal and the large houses at the bottom of Hill Road, soon converted into shops or banks.

83. A train to West Croydon, pulled by an engine called Merton, waiting in the station about 1880.

84. The start of the widening of the bridge in 1906 to enable two sets of tramlines to be laid across it. The chief addition was to come on the left or Raynes Park side. The addition on the right seems to have been for a pavement. Beyond the bridge the large houses have now had shops added to their fronts, while coal merchants have set up offices in the station forecourt.

was Alexander Maconochie. A Scotsman in his early forties and a civil servant at the Home Office, he bought a house in the recently developed Lingfield Road. A very ordinary two-storeyed building, it yet had a wonderful view (not then blocked by houses on the opposite side of the road) towards the Downs near Epsom, while at the end of the road was the Common and round the corner a wide variety of shops in the village. It was ideal for his wife and their six surviving children. It was also ideal for himself – a pleasant walk to the station down Sunnyside, across open fields (where Malcolm and Raymond Roads are today), over a stile at the bottom into a cart-track (now Worple Road) and so along the newly made-up St George's Road to the station where he would now find plenty of trains to take him to Waterloo (opened in 1848), followed by a short bus-ride to Whitehall.

Plenty of other professional men working in London followed his example. Sir Henry Peek MP regularly walked down the hill from Wimbledon House Parkside to catch the 8.50am train to London. Charles Grenside, a solicitor, walked even further to the station – from his house off Copse Hill. Such men liked the relatively quick journey to London and could afford the fare, while the country atmosphere of 'North Wimbledon' with its Common was a great attraction. So with their families many settled in large Victorian houses with pleasant gardens, especially in new roads south of the Ridgway, like Lansdowne and Arterberry. To help in the houses and gardens they needed servants and gardeners; to provide the supplies needed for their large meals and frequent parties, they required an assortment of shops with errand boys to deliver orders at the back door.

WORKING CLASS HOUSES

All these 'indispensable adjuncts to spacious late Victorian life' were provided by working-class families drawn to Wimbledon by the hope of finding a job. They came mostly from Inner London, the Home Counties and East Anglia, though some travelled from as far away as Devon, Scotland or Ireland. To house them, street after street of terraced houses went up – the first tentatively in the 1850s, a few more in the '60s and then the real rush in the '70s, '80s and '90s. By 1900 virtually all the fields on either side of the main line had been sold for building and a railway suburb had been created.

The first sign of this 'New Wimbledon' came, not by the station, but near Merton. The reason was the arrival there of an assured water-supply. On the top of the hill wells could be sunk easily in the gravel soil. Down in the valley even artesian wells were difficult to bore because of the thick belt of clay. In 1850, however, the Lambeth Water Company, using new cast-iron pipes, laid a ten-mile main from Thames Ditton (later from Staines Reservoir) to Brixton via New Malden, Raynes Park and South Wimbledon. For the first time it was possible for large numbers of people to live here and, as land prices were relatively cheap, developers decided to finance the building of blocks of small family houses (flats were felt to be out of place in a Victorian suburb).

The chief developers south of the Broadway were the National Freehold Land Society and its subsidiary, the British Land Company. They were

85. The station forecourt about 1900 with 'flys' (horse-drawn cabs) waiting for fares. In the centre is the London and South-Western booking-office, built in the 1880s. To its left is the District Railway terminus, opened in 1889. To the right is the bridge linking the platforms.

controlled by Liberal financiers who wanted, not merely to make a profit, but to increase the number of voters supporting their party at elections. They aimed to do this by buying land and selling it in small lots to men who would thus become 'forty shilling freeholders', the only people with the right to vote in county constituencies like East Surrey, which included Wimbledon (until it gained its own MP in 1885). Their first development in 1852 – a small 'Merton Estate' just north of the flour mill on the Wandle – only produced three rows of workmen's cottages along the unimaginatively named North, South and East Roads. But twenty years later in the early 1870s they were able to buy a large block of land south of the Broadway. Across it they laid out three streets going right down to the Kingston Road, named them after three Liberal Prime Ministers (Gladstone, Russell and Palmerston), got a surveyor to peg out plots, then advanced loans to local 'speculative builders' (so-called because they built 'on spec', with no prospective buyer in view). Builders like Thomas Batchelor and John Smith (both living in the newly developed Hartfield Road) put up blocks of terraced houses, all with similarly-designed fronts. At the same time the Society was financing other developments – along Haydons Road and on new streets to the east (like Gilbert, Hubert and De

Burgh Roads). At times so many houses were being built that the supply outpaced demand. In the late 1870s and early '80s during 'a general depression of trade', it was reported that 'a large number of houses in South Wimbledon are unoccupied at present'.

Most other developers, however, were chiefly interested in profit. In 1854 a 'Church of England Estate' (so named because two of the men financing it were clergymen) was laid out at the bottom of the Merton Road. Along the new Southey, Griffiths, Pelham and Montague Roads, large semidetached houses were built, some with coach houses and basements for servants. Like the homes off the Ridgway, they were bought by prosperous middle-class men – barristers, architects, stockbrokers, publishers, even a vellum binder and an oil broker. But the plots sold slowly and many were not built on until the 1890s. Far more important was the development from 1880 onwards of the large Cowdrey Farm estate. Its fields, covering 340 acres north of the Broadway from Haydons Road to the main line railway, were sold in 1872, but building for some reason was delayed. No record seems to exist of the identity of the developers, but they were certainly not the British Land Company to judge from the names given to the roads: Queens, Kings, Princes and Stanley.

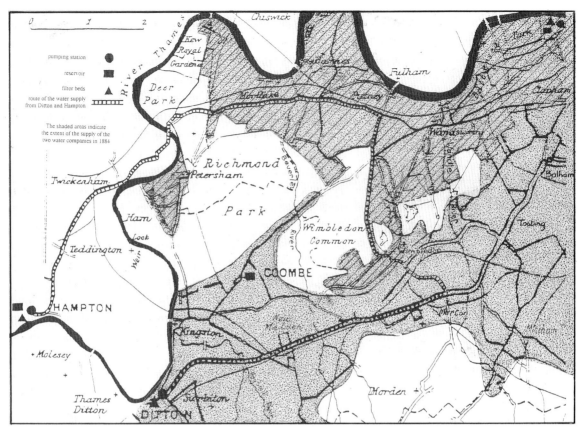

86. A map of Wimbledon's water supply in 1884. It came from two sources: for New Wimbledon from Thames Ditton, in pipes laid by the Lambeth Water Company in 1850; seven years later for the Village from Hampton, via the Southwark and Vauxhall Company's pipes.

Builders like James Crouch and Harry Johnson put up large middle-class 'semis', as well as more working-class terraced houses. At the same time, west of the line to Croydon, other developers were laying out the Dundonald estate to house more working-class families, while just above Kingston Road John Innes was developing Kingswood and Mayfield Roads as part of his Merton Park estate.

Of all the developments , however, perhaps the most imaginative was one between Hartfield and Gladstone Roads, known as Bertram Cottages. There were sixteen of these 'model cottages', designed by a local engineer, H.C. Forde, and paid for by Keziah Peache, a lady who lived in Church Road and used the fortune she inherited from her father (owner of Belvedere House) on works of charity. Started in 1867, they were completed in five years, as the date 'A.D. 1872' with the initials 'K.P.' outlined in red brick on the fronts of two of them proudly proclaim. They were let at low rents to poorer families of 'good character and cleanly habits'. Among the first residents were a railway plate-layer from Norfolk (with three lodgers including a porter and a railway clerk), a whitesmith from Brixton and a bricklayer from Essex. All were young men with families; none had been born in Wimbledon.

Such families were typical of the residents of New Wimbledon. They were mostly young manual workers whose jobs were local – on the railway, on building sites, as tradesmen, or up the hill as servants in one of the big houses. They may have come here by train, but they were not commuters as they could not afford the expense of a daily fare. Mr Clark who lived here in the 1890s, for instance, was paid just over a pound a week for working at the railway sidings just above Dundonald Road as a blacksmith's assistant. His hours were from 6.00am to 5.30pm six days a week; he was allowed no tea breaks and threatened with the sack if he smoked at work. But at least he had a steady job and a reasonable house.

87. Cows grazing in a field below the Broadway in the 1860s. The right of way behind them later became Palmerston Road. In the background are the first houses of Griffith and Pelham Roads.

88. Dundonald Road about 1910, with Dundonald Elementary School (opened in 1894) in the centre. The road (once known as Lower Worple, a right of way to the fields) had been developed thirty years earlier, with a number of small roads next to the railway goods depot. Beyond, a large recreation ground was created on land once part of Merton Hall Farm.

89. *Haydons Road about 1910 with the British Queen public house at the corner of North Road, a number of small shops opposite and a major tram route recently started to Summerstown. The working-class homes here had been built in the 1880s, but the road was old and had an important farm on its western side, managed in the 1760s and '70s by George Heydon.*

Conditions were worse for those living in the Haydons Road area, described in one report as 'the poorest in the district'. The houses were often badly built with faulty drains and a contaminated water supply. Many were overcrowded, with lodgers taken in to help pay the bills. The men were frequently faced with unemployment, especially during hard winters. In 1882, for instance, when 'there was great scarcity of work for many weeks', a local painter with a wife and eight children was suddenly 'thrown out of work' and then contracted rheumatic fever. His family were said to have been 'literally starving and the children ill from lack of food' when saved by a Wimbledon charity.

Such poor children were the chief sufferers in New Wimbledon. They were easy victims of infectious diseases, especially diphtheria, typhoid and scarlet fever. In 1899 'the many cases' of diphtheria were put down to 'faulty drains', while scarlet fever caused the closure of one local school

for a fortnight. The Medical Officer of Health ascribed the recent increase in Wimbledon's death-rate to 'a great change in the character of the district'. Whereas forty years earlier most of the population had lived 'on the north or highest side' of the parish, 'now houses have been rapidly built over the south, in many parts low-lying and water-logged', leading to a death-rate double that on top of the hill.

His remarks highlight one aspect of the amazing transformation that had come over the area in just half a century. The census of 1851 listed a mere 2,693 people living in the parish, almost all in or near the old village. Fifty years later the number had risen to 41,652, nearly sixteen times more, with well over half of them now living south of the railway. This sudden, dramatic expansion posed serious problems on a scale never faced by the old Manor Court or Vestry, and the challenge had to be met by local people with little help from central government.

The Victorian Broadway

ORIGIN OF ITS NAME

The places where the challenge posed by the sudden growth of a New Wimbledon was met most effectively were all situated along a road right in its heart, the Broadway. One of the area's oldest highways, it had for centuries been a country lane running between hedges, with cows grazing or corn ripening in the fields beyond. Known as 'the lane to Merton', it had been traversed by farmers in their carts, travellers on horseback, poor families in search of work and once by a King, the seriously ill Henry VIII, in December 1546.

The first houses ever to go up along this road were those of the stationmaster and railway policeman to the south of the new railway in 1838. They were not followed by any others for the next 25 years. Then in the 1870s the west side below the new Prince of Wales pub was quickly developed and lined by small shops and large private houses, followed in the succeeding decade by others on the opposite side. A few fields managed to survive until the early years of the next century, notably just below Latimer Road where St Winefride's church was not built until 1905. Otherwise in under half a century a country lane had been transformed into an urban thoroughfare.

The name Broadway for this old road has a curious history. It seems to have originated at the time the Local Board Offices were built on the site of the stationmaster's house in 1878. The Offices must have been well back from the old frontage, leaving a wide area for the road, soon called 'The Broad Way'. The rest of the road was named in maps or local directories either the 'New Wimbledon Road' or simply 'Merton Road'. In the 1880s the term 'Broadway' began creeping southwards – and in an unusual way. A local directory of 1900 lists the shops on the west side up to about Gladstone Road as 'the Broadway', whereas those on the opposite side (apart from a few immediately below the Board Offices) were listed as in 'Merton Road'. In the present century the name progressed southward until by the early 1930s the Broadway on both sides had been extended as far as the bend by Latimer Road, where it remains today.

90. *Holy Trinity Church in the late 1860s, when it was the only building on the north side of the Broadway. With its large vicarage, it stood on marshy ground near the fields of Cowdrey Farm. It was partly reconstructed in the 1970s.*

HOLY TRINITY

Far more important, however, than the strange evolution of its name was the part four buildings on the Broadway played in the struggle to improve the lives of the 'immigrants' to New Wimbledon. The first was Holy Trinity, the original Anglican 'chapel of ease' below the hill. Opened in 1862 just as the Pelham Road estate opposite was growing, its first Vicar, the Revd William Bartlett, organised a series of charities, designed more to help poor families in the Haydons Road area than those nearer the church. They included a New Wimbledon and Merton Soup Kitchen ('to supply the poor, such as reside south of the railroad, with good soup during the winter months'), a Medical Dispensary ('to supply gratuitous medical assistance and medicines'), a Maternal Society ('to help with medical aid and linen at the confinement of poor women of good character, resident in Wimbledon for at least a year'), a Clothing, Bedding and Fuel Club ('for the benefit of respectable labourers and their families'), as well as schools for infants, primary boys and girls, youths already out at work, and an Emigration Society for the unemployed. Bartlett's work was continued by his successors at Holy Trinity and partly imitated in soup kitchens organised by local traders in the cold winters of 1886 and 1895, and also in the Wimbledon Charity Organisation (now the Wimbledon Guild) which gave hundreds of 'tickets' to 'deserving poor' to enable them to get a ration of bread.

91. *The Revd William Bartlett (1832-95), the first vicar at Holy Trinity. As well as serving his many poor parishioners, he found time to write Wimbledon's first full local history. In 1868 he moved to a parish in Sussex, where he spent the rest of his life.*

92. *The offices of the Local Board of Health, in about 1910. By then they had become Wimbledon's first Town Hall. They were pulled down in 1929.*

A NEW TOWN HALL

Charity, even on this scale, was clearly not enough to deal with the many problems in New Wimbledon. A more effective type of local government was needed to take over from the Vestry. It was provided at the second important building in the Broadway, the Local Board Offices just below the southern entrance to the station. A Local Board of Health had been set up in Wimbledon twelve years earlier, primarily to deal with sanitation, 'nuisances' (such as cesspools) and infectious diseases. For a time the Vestry continued to discuss local affairs, but gradually they lost their powers, especially over new roads, housebuilding and the water supply, and in the end were confined to their original business, church affairs. As a result, the Board had to employ more paid officials, and so decided to move down the hill from their old office in the High Street to the new building at the top of the Broadway.

The Offices were later described as 'an eyesore which lets down the whole town'. For fifty years, however, they were the centre for growing civic pride. The Board, made up of fifteen members elected by the ratepayers and chaired by men as distinguished as the Headmaster of Wimbledon School, the Revd John Brackenbury, discussed a wide variety of local problems. In 1886, for instance, these ranged from the effect of recent snowstorms to the need to water the roads during the summer. But their chief work was to set up a number of new, vital services: a Sewage Works in water-meadows by the Wandle, two Hospitals

93. A parade of the Volunteer Fire Brigade on 18 July 1900, going up Hill Road and about to pass Elys Corner. Two steam fire-engines lead a Carnival procession of floats and two military bands. They were raising money to help the families of soldiers fighting in the Boer War.

for Infectious Diseases in Durnsford Road, a new Burial Ground at Gap Road, a Volunteer Fire Brigade which operated from a station behind the Board Offices, a 'Free Library', opened in Hill Road after bitter controversy and the first Public Recreation Ground off Haydons Road. In 1894 the Board became an Urban District Council with the same officials and largely the same members, but elected on a wider franchise. Their chief improvement was the momentous decision to build their own Power Station at Durnsford Road and to light local streets with electric lamps rather than oil. By 1900 as a result of all these changes New Wimbledon had become a rather pleasanter and certainly healthier place in which to live.

It was also rather more law-abiding thanks to the work based at a third important building – the Police Station. Opened about 1870 in one of the new houses just beyond the site of the future Victoria Crescent (made in 1887 to celebrate the Queen's Golden Jubilee), it was staffed by a sergeant and eight constables. They were kept busy (as the weekly police court reports in the local paper show) dealing with men 'drunk and disorderly', costermongers 'obstructing the Broadway', owners of 'dangerous dogs' and a man from Tooting driving a carriage without lights and trying to bribe the policeman not to report him.

Finally, at 28 The Broadway an attempt was made to follow the example of the Village Club on the top of the hill and provide a club for 'working men'. Known as the South Wimbledon Club and supported by local dignitaries, it was founded in the late 1880s and provided 'reading, chess, card and billiard rooms', as well as 'a quoits ground' and 'refreshments of all kinds at moderate prices'. It was said to be 'social and non-political'. How successful it was is not known, but it still existed in the 1930s, though by then it had moved to Russell Road.

THE BROADWAY SHOPS

There can, however, be no doubt about the success of the shops that by 1900 lined the Broadway. They played an important part in brightening life in New Wimbledon, as well as providing plenty of jobs for the 'immigrants'. The first few seem to have been opened about 1867 just below the corner of Hartfield Road (where the Prince of Wales pub was to be built in 1870). Among them were a butcher's (run by Richard Way who later moved to near Raynes Park station), a confectioner's and a greengrocer's.   The only large department store seems to have been Skewes on the corner of Gladstone Road (replaced by Woolworth's in 1935).   It sold drapery and furniture and packed its windows with goods, especially hats which in Victorian times everyone wore.

The shopkeepers' offered a highly competitive service – 'Families waited upon daily at their own residences'; 'van and barrows deliver all through Wimbledon'; 'repairs on the shortest notice'; 'a postcard will receive prompt attention' (at a time when there no telephones and a card posted in the morning was delivered that same afternoon). There was in fact no need for a lady to visit a grocer, baker or butcher. The shopkeeper or his roundsman called at the back door for orders; an errand boy soon brought the goods on his bicycle.

For those who preferred to go shopping in person, there was plenty of choice.   At 14 The Broadway Hewitt and Son, 'Merchant Taylors', offered men's suits from thirteen shillings and eleven pence, and 'a special line in men's trousers' at three and eleven pence, while opposite at 49 near the Council Offices, J. Pierce ('established 1879') advertised men's suits at 32/6d, with trousers at 8/11d.   At number 6 A. Love, ('established 1871') 'Family Baker and Pastry Cook', claimed to sell 'the very best and purest bread that can be purchased in Surrey' and at his Refreshment Rooms to provide 'the best cup of tea that can be obtained in the district'.   Opposite him at 42 were Haynes Brothers, 'Cash Grocers', whose window displayed 'the finest tea and coffee', while almost next door at 44 was the American Teeth Company advertising 'stoppings' at 3/6d, extractions for just a shilling and 'a partial set' of false teeth for a guinea. Already in the Broadway were branches of famous firms, including the Victoria Wine Company, the Home and Colonial Stores and Lipton's 'Tea Stores'.

Unlike the Georgian shops in the High Street, none of the Victorian buildings in the Broadway were of much architectural merit.   Only those in the curved terrace on the corner with Queens Road gain a mention in the Victorian Society's guide to the area. But, at least unlike the shops north of the bridge, they have not yet been swept away in the cause of redevelopment or, like the town's best known department store Elys, been hideously modernised.   A hundred years ago the 700 or so shops north as well as south of the railway had already made Wimbledon a good shopping centre, 'catering (according to a local guide book) for the wants of the district in a manner equal to the best London shops at competitive prices'.

94. *The top of the Broadway just below the railway bridge about 1910. The horse bus has just started its journey to Putney. Traffic is otherwise confined to carts, barrows and bicycles, with no sign of a car.*

95. *The Prince of Wales public house about 1910 with plenty of traffic on the recently widened bridge over the railway. The horse-drawn 'fly' on the left is going into the station forecourt. The tram is going to Tooting. The young cyclist does not appear to be worried by the tram-tracks, while the carriage on the right seems to be on the wrong side of the road.*

Inns, Beerhouses and Temperance Taverns

PUBS IN THE VILLAGE

By the end of the nineteenth century the Broadway had a wide selection of shops, but only one public house, The Prince of Wales. Constructed about 1870 by James Crouch (who also put up houses in Queens Road and Wimbledon Park), it is still an imposing building, dominating the bridge and the neighbouring shops. From the start it was described as a Railway Hotel (presumably for passengers using the southern entrance to the station) and followed the fashion set on the other side of the bridge by The South-Western Railway Hotel (originally The Mansel Arms) and soon copied by The Raynes Park Hotel, opened in 1874, three years after the station.

Railway hotels were a new name for buildings once known as alehouses or taverns or inns or even beerhouses. An alehouse was the original public house where ale and later beer were brewed and sold on the premises – and vetted by the local Ale-conner to see if they were up to standard. A tavern

was the next development, a more select establishment where wine as well as ale and beer were sold. An inn was the inevitable result of the growth of trade and improvements in main roads;   it provided food as well as drink, along with rooms to lodge in for the night and stables for the horses (or a change of horse). Finally a beerhouse was a short-lived Victorian experiment, originating in an Act of 1830 which allowed any ratepayer who could afford two guineas excise duty to brew and sell beer on his premises without having to get a licence from the local JPs.

All these different types of public house (a term which itself was not used until the eighteenth century) duly appeared in the village and with few other sources of entertainment, farmers, tradesmen and labourers relied on the pub for refreshment and relaxation. There, before a good fire, they could enjoy a drink with their friends, perhaps smoke a long 'churchwarden' pipe, play at cards or dice (both strictly illegal) or join in a game of bowls on a green at the back. Apart from the parish church, pubs were the most used buildings in the village.

So the men (or women) who managed them, known as 'victuallers' or 'tavern-keepers' or 'tippulatores' (the Latin word used in Manor Court documents), were important local personalities. They were also often in trouble. In the early years of Elizabeth I's reign Robert Collins was frequently fined for allowing his customers 'to play at illegal

96. The King's Head, Merton High Street, about 1902, with its distinguished Georgian front (sadly modernised in the 1930s). The posters and the pram are typical of the Edwardian era.

games' and for having 'people of bad character in his house'. A century later under Charles II Samuel Beakes was accused of 'having his alehouse open during the hours of divine service on Sunday'. The customers as well often appeared in court, none more frequently than Tobias Barton, a blacksmith. In the 1680s he was charged with making himself a public nuisance: 'a common disturber of the peace and stirrer up of discords', 'throwing a large quantity of dung into Le Pond' and 'levying money under cover of the law, having no lawful authority'.

Alehouses appear in the village during the Middle Ages. The first with a name is listed in the 1617 survey – The White Hart in Church Lane, run by a widow, Mrs Letchworth. By the middle of the eighteenth century it had been replaced by The Red Lyon which was closed by local magistrates in 1755 because of 'misdemeanours such as the suffering of playing of cards and dice on the Sabbath day, to the encouragement of vice'. In its turn it was followed by The Swan which also closed before the end of the century, along with the village's two other alehouses, both on Westside. The original Crooked Billet (which goes back no

further than the 1740s) had to close in 1794 when its owner, Thomas Wray, died. The Rising Sun, on the other hand, like The Red Lyon was shut down by the JPs on the grounds that it was 'destructive of morals and injurious to the good order of society'. A number of poor labourers living near by petitioned for its licence to be restored, but the building became (and remains) a private house.

By 1800 only three public houses survived in the parish. Two were in the village – The Dog and Fox, and The Rose and Crown; the third was on the boundary with Merton, The King's Head. All had probably started as taverns, but had graduated into becoming inns. The King's Head claimed to be the oldest, 'established in 1496', but there seem to be no documents to prove the date. It was certainly an important inn on the main road to Epsom, but was only of concern to people in the village as a 'refuelling stop' when the bounds were being beaten.

The Dog and Fox may have been even older, as a tavern was probably on the site opposite the corner of the High Street and Church Lane during the late Middle Ages. But the first certain record of an inn there dates from the survey of 1617. It was then known as My Lord's Arms, presumably with a signboard bearing the heraldic arms of the lord of the manor, the Earl of Exeter. It had 'eight rooms, two butteries, two barns, a stable and a yard', and like The White Hart down Church Lane was run by a widow, Mary Walker. Its present name only appears in 1758; before then it was referred to as 'Mr Winchester's' after the innkeeper who ran the pub from 1748 to 1783. Under him, meetings of the Vestry (of which he was a member) were often held there. During the Napoleonic Wars, the Volunteers were trained 'in their military discipline' by an Army Sergeant on the bowling green at the back. The inn was then 'a low, white building, two storeyed'. It was completely reconstructed in 1868 by the leading builders in the village, Parsons and Townsend, and enlarged again in the present century as the Wimbledon Hill Hotel.

The origin of its rival, The Rose and Crown, is rather later. The deeds of Eagle House show that it was established about 1650 during the Commonwealth by the Puritan owner, Sir Richard Betenson. Known at first as The Rose, the extra words 'and Crown' could only be added after the Restoration of Charles II. Its first innkeeper, Thomas Heburne, is the only Wimbledon tradesman known to have issued trade tokens, small unofficial coins which helped to make up for a shortage of change. In 1666 he was burgled, probably by one of the servants, who stole 'six hens, one cheese, one cheese-cloth and one stool' but was soon captured and sent to a House of Correction. The inn was clearly a large one, taxed on five hearths in the 1660s, but the present building with its twin roof seems to date from the eighteenth century.

By then it had become 'a genteel inn', the favourite meeting place of the Vestry. Its dining-room was also used for the Friendly Society's annual Whitsun banquet, as well as for churchwardens' dinners. On such occasions innkeepers like Samuel Mason (who ran it from 1772 to 1793, as well as carrying on his trade as a carpenter) could provide huge meals. One for the Dean of Croydon on his visitation of the parish included a round of beef, veal, hams, 'puding, vagatebls', bread, cheese and butter, tarts, wine, punch, 'suger, lemmonds,' brandy, tea, beer and tobacco, all recorded on a bill with one of the village's first printed headings. From 1780 the inn was also the starting-point for 'the Wimbledon Machine', the first public short-stage coach to London. It ran every Monday, Wednesday and Friday, and took two hours to reach Charing Cross via Putney Bridge.

Fifty years later the successors of Edward

97. *The Crooked Billet, about 1885.*

98. The Dog and Fox in 1868, with its Georgian front, probably added to an earlier building. Painting by J.E. Wilson.

Winchester and Samuel Mason were up in arms at the passing of the Beer Houses Act which brought free trade to brewing and inn-keeping. They were faced with serious competition for the first time since the 1790s. A trade directory of 1832 shows that five 'Beer Shops' had already opened in Wimbledon. Three soon disappeared, but were replaced by three others. By the time of the 1841 census there were nine – two in the High Street, two in the Crooked Billet, two more round West View and individual ones in Church Lane, the Ridgway and Durnsford Road. They were very popular as their beer was cheaper and it could be taken away to be drunk at home. 'Respectable' people were horrified. Beerhouses were seen as 'sources of sedition' and attacks on 'the evils of drink' became as common as during the gin plague a hundred years earlier. So in 1869 Parliament passed another Act forcing beerhouses to get a licence from JPs like other pubs. Many were refused, but a few secured a full publican's licence.

Among them were some of the best known pubs in modern Wimbledon. In Church Lane The Castle started about 1840 as a beerhouse run by John Steptoe. Next door it had a rival, The Jolly Butchers, which it later bought up. In the Ridgway The King of Denmark is the successor of The Jolly Gardeners, also set up about 1840 by Charles Deacon, a

99. The Rose and Crown in 1913. The building with its twin roof seems to date from the eighteenth century.

carpenter, to serve the poor labourers living in South Road (behind where Thornton Hill is to-day). The Crooked Billet was resurrected in the 1830s by William Williams, a young man, described in the census of 1851 as 'retailer of beer and coals', while The Hand in Hand is said to have started as a bakery in the 1850s and only began to sell beer in the 1870s, when its owner, Mrs Holland, took out one of the new licences. Finally, The Fox and Grapes in Almshouse Lane (now Camp Road) originated in 1837 as a Union Beershop run by William Fisher and did not adopt its present name until about twenty years later.

TEMPERANCE CAMPAIGN

This 'pub explosion' was nation-wide. Within six months of the passing of the Beer Houses Act in 1830 the number of places selling beer had gone up by fifty per cent. There was widespread alarm at the consequent increase in drunkenness and teetotalism became a major national issue. A strong temperance movement developed, led by the Nonconformist Temperance Mission and the Anglican Temperance Society (whose patron was the Queen). They aimed to promote not merely moderation in drinking, but reform of 'the intemperate' and removal of everything which led to drunkenness.

In Wimbledon the campaign won many supporters, above all the Vicar, Canon Haygarth. As president of the local branch of the Anglican Temperance Society, he presided at a meeting in the Lecture Hall of the Village Club in March 1868. In his speech he declared that 'intoxication is our most baneful national sin' and that 'in this parish the evils of drink are too apparent'. His remedy was 'a glass of water' which 'if at hand' would lead 'working-men to refrain from a public house'. So he persuaded those at the meeting to support the erection of a drinking-fountain at the top of Wimbledon Hill in memory of Joseph Toynbee, a leading ear, nose and throat specialist and a founder of the Village Club, who had died suddenly two years earlier. Haygarth also led his fellow clergy in 'a special mission' to all the local public houses and beershops. Such actions, however, seem to have had little effect.

Seemingly more effective, at least for a time, was the work of the Van Sommer family, fervent Evangelicals who lived at South Lodge on Southside. James, a solicitor, and his mother promoted a rival attraction to the pub – a coffee tavern. Backed by Canon Haygarth and leading residents like Charles Arnold and Thurstan Holland, they opened the first, named The Welcome, right opposite The Dog and Fox in 1877. It provided

100. Canon Henry Haygarth (1821-1902), vicar of Wimbledon from 1859 until his death. A conservative in his religious views, he promoted and helped to finance the building of extra Anglican churches and schools, especially in New Wimbledon. He lived for his parish – and for his garden with its fine display of roses.

the patrons with 'reading and coffee rooms, good beds, a club room, a lending library, a slate club and a penny bank'. It was open all day from 5.30am to 11pm and its satisfied customers were said to have made 'frequent favourable remarks upon the quality of the tea, coffee and cocoa'. So a second coffee tavern was opened two years later in Denmark Road, just off the Ridgway – and near the new King of Denmark. In 1881 an even more ambitious scheme was launched – to rival The Alexandra public house and The Prince of Wales railway hotel at the bottom of the hill by setting up a Wimbledon Coffee Palace and Temperance Hotel on the corner of St George's Road. Not only were 'working men' catered for, but local societies were encouraged to hold meetings there rather than at a pub. Quite a number did, including the Spencer Cricket Club, Mid-Surrey Cyclists, the Society of Painters and the Poultry Club.

Within a few years, however, reports on the coffee taverns were not so rosy. In 1886 receipts at the Denmark Road shop were 'much reduced by the general depression of trade and during the winter months business has been very slack'; four years later it had to close. The Coffee Palace near the station did valiant work providing soup 'among working classes in distress', but it too was soon forced to close for lack of enough customers. By 1900 only the original Welcome was still surviving and even this had to shut its doors a few years later, despite the support of the Wimbledon and Merton United Temperance Council, in which Anglicans, Methodists, Baptists and Congregationalists co-operated for the first time.

Not a single public house seems to have closed as a result of their propaganda. Yet they were not discouraged. In February 1916 the Anglican Temperance Society opened a new coffee tavern in the High Street on the corner of Lancaster Road and named it The Welcome. It later became St Mary's Parish Hall.

101. The Welcome Café at the corner of the High Street and Church Road about 1890. Its manager, customers, spectators and a village policeman stand in front of the shop, which survives today though used for a very different business.

102. *The Toynbee Fountain, photographed about 1890 in its original position at the junction of the Ridgway, High Street and Wimbledon Hill. The hay cart on the right is passing the fence and trees at the edge of the Belvedere estate. The building beyond is the bank at Church Road corner.*

Worple Road and its Centre Court

ALL-ENGLAND GROUND

Fear of the effects of drink was not confined to temperance crusaders. Developers were very conscious of the effect a pub could have on the 'tone' of a neighbourhood. So, starting with John Augustus Beaumont and 'the Covenant' which he insisted on including in every one of his land sales in Wimbledon Park, they wrote into the deeds of middle-class houses all over the district a clause banning the purchaser from carrying on 'the trade of an innkeeper, victualler or retailer of wine, spirits or beer' at the property, along with any 'noxious or offensive manufacture'. This explains why people living on or near Worple Road have to go to Hill Road or Raynes Park to find a pub or an off-licence.

The development of Worple Road was in any case rather unusual. For centuries it had been a quiet cart-track through fields with picturesque names like Upper and Lower White Hart, and Little and Great Ladies. Known in Tudor times as 'Warpell Way' (meaning a right of way which must never be ploughed up), it led nowhere and finally petered out near The Downs, a much more important right of way, linking Wimbledon and Merton Commons. Old folk, remembering their childhood in the early years of Queen Victoria's reign, declared that 'often the carts sank into it and were pulled out again with some difficulty'. They also recalled going blackberrying there and once seeing a hunt chase a fox down the road and over Mr Thomson's Nursery wall at the end. As late as 1874 a most atmospheric painting by Emily Bardswell shows 'Middle Worple Lane' just beyond the bottom of Thornton Hill. It is still a narrow earth track overhung by trees; in the middle a shepherd leads his sheep to pasture. Yet, hidden by the hedge on the left, there was a large field which in three years' time was to be the scene of the first All-England Lawn Tennis Championships.

This four acre field between the road and the railway had been leased in 1869 by the newly founded All-England Croquet Club. The members needed the cheapest possible ground; after a long search they found it – on Worple Lane. They laid out twelve croquet lawns (despite the intrusion of cows and pigs from the neighbouring Southdown Farm) and were allowed to use a footpath by the railway line to reach the ground from the station. They then held their first Croquet

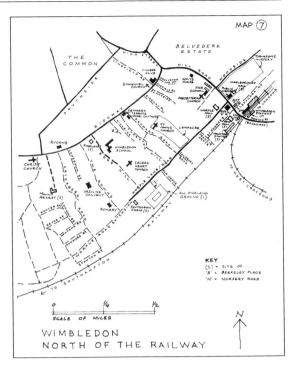

103. *A map of Wimbledon north of the railway, drawn by John Wallace.*

Championship. Within a few years, however, the game seemed to be losing its popularity and, at the suggestion of a member, one of the lawns was set aside for a new sport, lawn tennis. Soon four more lawns were needed and in July 1877 the Club decided to hold its first Lawn Tennis Championships, using all the croquet lawns. Twenty-two men took part (women were not allowed to do so for another seven years). Competitors paid a guinea to enter, but had to 'provide their own rackets and wear shoes without heels'. Spectators were charged a shilling to get in. The umpires wore top hats and sat on low platforms. The final had to be postponed four times, first because of the Eton and Harrow match at Lords on the Saturday and then because it rained on the following Monday, Tuesday and Wednesday. It finally took place in damp, overcast conditions on the Thursday before a crowd of two thousand and was won in three straight sets by Spencer Gore, a local sportsman who had been brought up at Westside House on the Common and was in fact far happier playing cricket.

By the early 1880s the Championships were making a small profit. Soon so many wanted to see the final (despite a rise in the entry fee to two shillings and sixpence) that in 1884 a permanent

104. *Worple Road in 1874, painted by Emily Bardswell.*

105. *Tennis at the Worple Road ground in 1880. The road is to the left of the courts, the railway to the right. The thatched summer houses were meant for lady spectators.*

106. *Worple Road and the All-England ground from the air in 1919. Above the road is the Roman Catholic Church of the Sacred Heart and Wimbledon College field. On the far left are the large houses along The Downs.*

stand was built for the Centre Court and tarpaulin covers were used to protect all the courts from the inevitable rain. In the 1890s the Doherty brothers drew large crowds and then overseas players began to dominate the finals. By the reign of Edward VII 'Wimbledon' had become a major event in the social calendar along with Lords, Ascot and Henley. Tea on the lawn in front of the pavilion gave it a garden party atmosphere. Tickets were in such demand that for the first time all-night queues stretched up Nursery Road and during the day extended along Worple Road. The Championships of 1913 were especially crowded. 10,000 spectators crammed in on finals day and cars and taxis blocked neighbouring streets. The residents complained and the Club Committee realised the tournament would have to move, but the outbreak of war delayed the change until 1922. Their old ground has survived (as the sports field of Wimbledon High School), as has the old pavilion and at the entrance are a pair of ornamental gates which commemorate the long association between Worple Road and lawn tennis.

BUILDING ALONG THE ROAD

As the first Championships began, the development of the road was already under way. It had been launched at the eastern end near Hill Road by a 33-year-old builder, Henry Harmer. The youngest son of a carpenter and builder, he had started work at his father's yard in Lingfield Road. In 1870 he moved to a new house which he had built on the unmade Worple Lane, just before its junction with Francis Grove. He opened his own yard and estate office on the opposite side and, with a workforce of forty to fifty men and nine boys, began building large detached middle-class houses along the south side and in new side roads, especially Courthope Villas (with a very convenient brickfield just behind). Until the late 1890s the houses had names rather than numbers which must have made life difficult for the postman. In less than fifteen years Harmer had reached the area of the lawn tennis ground. Beyond there were still fields owned by the Southdown Farm, run by Messrs Freeth and Pocock. In regular advertisements on the front page of local papers, they claimed to supply 'the richest milk and cream' from ' a superior herd of shorthorn and Jersey cows' and sold it at their 'creamery' at 50 Hill Road. The farm did not disappear until the early years of the present century, while Henry Harmer survived until 1926, 'a quiet and retiring gentleman' who never married.

The only other builder known to be living along Worple Road in the last years of Queen Victoria's reign was Alfred Crocker – on the north side near Darlaston Road. He put up large three-storeyed houses in that road, as well as others on the western side of Edge Hill, but does not seem to have been responsible for those opposite Harmer's. The first development here seems to have been at the end near Hill Road in 1878. The Wimbledon Estate Company, with an office on the corner opposite Elys, built large middle-class houses with gardens in front from near Worple Mews to Raymond Road (or Mansel as it was then known). They were bought by men like George Ely, a successful grocer in Hill Road, and William Santo Crimp, the Local Board's engineer in the 1880s who cured the nasty smells from the drains by designing 'Wimbledon columns' (large tubes which dispelled the smell well above human level). Other builders put up similar houses beyond Darlaston as far as Arterberry. But there in the 1880s the road came to a full stop. The only way to get to Raynes Park was to go over a stile and cross fields to Worple Road West, laid out in the 1850s, but still without any buildings.

107. Thomas Devas (1814-1900). He played an important part in the setting up of the Village Club and the building of Christ Church, as well as serving on the Local Board. He is commemorated locally in the name of Devas Road, as are his sons-in-law in Conway and Hunter Roads.

108. Arterberry Road, 5 May 1911. Devas laid out the road (named after local fields) in 1873 and sold plots for large houses on its eastern side. The road was given a series of bends to enable horses and carts to go up and down more easily, helped by the stretch of rough earth on the right where drivers could use a skid pan more effectively.

109. John Townsend (1823-1917), Chairman of the Local Board from 1885 to 1894.

The fields were part of the large Mount Ararat estate which extended from the Ridgway down the hill to the railway. Its owner was Thomas Devas, Managing Director of a textile firm. To pay off his mortgage on the property, he had already laid out Arterberry Road with sizeable mansions on its eastern side – and a horse trough at the bottom. He was quite ready to allow Worple Road to be extended across his land, but several members of the Local Board, especially its chairman, John Townsend, a leading builder, suspected that his main aim was personal profit. In fact the people who felt they would profit most were those in Cottenham Park who complained of being cut off from the shops in Wimbledon. In a petition they claimed that during a recent fire the engine from Kingston had reached the blaze more quickly than the Wimbledon one from the Broadway.

In the end after a long and acrimonious debate the Board decided to build 'the Worple Road Extension'. This was constructed at a cost of just over £1000 and was formally opened on 13 May 1891. The members of the Board drove there in a procession of horse-drawn carriages, accompanied by mounted police, three local bands and the Board's three steam fire-engines (one, 'the May Queen' just 'christened'). At the junction with Arterberry they were met by carts and cabs, decorated with flags and bunting, all full of people blowing whistles, shouting and waving. In the evening the Board celebrated with a dinner in St George's Hall.

TRAMS AND SHOPPING

Whether the celebrations would have been quite so enthusiastic had its supporters seen Worple Road today is a matter of debate. Certainly within a few years a quiet suburban lane was transformed into a major thoroughfare. First, in the early 1900s semi-detached houses were built on both sides between Arterberry and Pepys Roads. Then, after a five year delay needed to widen the road and lay the tracks, trams arrived from Kingston in 1907 (soon followed by horse buses). Their fares were cheaper and the service was more frequent than on the trains, so more people decided to move into

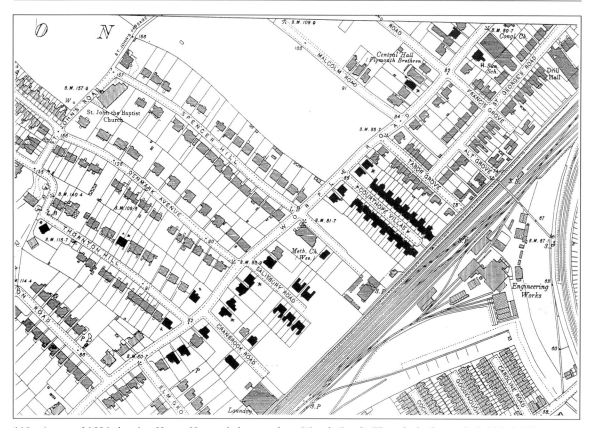

110. A map of 1894 showing Henry Harmer's houses along Worple Road. Those he built are shaded black. His own house is marked with an H.

the area and new houses began to go up along side roads off both the new Extension and the previously deserted Worple Road West.

Wives took the tram to go shopping in Wimbledon, especially at Elys 'Taylor's, Mercer's and Draper's Store' (founded 1876) whose sales shot up after the conductors were induced by gifts such as a pullover to shout 'Elys Corner' at the right stop.   Husbands could use it to go to meetings at the new Worple Hall on the opposite side of the road (where in 1907 a speech by Bertrand Russell in favour of votes for women was disrupted by rats, deliberately set free among the audience), or to Wimbledon's first cinema, 'The Electric Theatre' (later renamed The Queen's), opened in 1910 on the other side of Worple Mews. The trams were also useful for children going to schools along the road (like Wimbledon Collegiate by the Mews or St George's near Spencer Hill – neither of which still exists) or to others up the hill (such as Wimbledon College, Rokeby or the Ursuline Convent – all of which have now cel-

ebrated their centenary). The whole family could catch the tram to visit one of the many doctors or dentists whose surgeries soon lined the road. Churchgoers too benefited, with Congregational and Methodist churches along the road by the middle 1880s, soon followed just to the north by Trinity Presbyterian church and the first Roman Catholic church since the Reformation.

The nearest Anglican church, St Mark's, was straight opposite the Hill end of the road down a cul-de-sac. Built in 1880 just as Worple Road was being developed, it effectively blocked the creation here of a crossroad which might later have eased the traffic problem. Instead a crossroad had already been made to the south when Alexandra Road was laid out in the mid-1870s, opposite St George's Road, then far more important than Worple. This crossroad only came into its own just over a century later when cars and lorries were diverted off the end of Worple Road and on to St George's, and the old buildings round the crossing were redeveloped.

111. *Joseph Ely's shop in Worple Road in 1904,with Russell's studio to the right.*

112. *Russell's shop was cut in half on 8 August 1906 to enable a double tram track to be laid.*

113. *Laying tramlines along Worple Road in 1906. On the left is the western end of Stanton Road; on the right houses are being built just before the junction with Langham Road.*

Cottenham Park and the road to Kingston

THE RIDGWAY

The Worple Road Extension proved as important for the future of Cottenham Park as its supporters had predicted. Until 1891, while developments took place elsewhere, the area had largely been by-passed. Situated between two ancient highways to Kingston – one from Merton, the other from Wimbledon village – it had for centuries been covered by woods or by 'bramble, thorn and furze'. Only after 1757, when the owners of Prospect Place began to tame the northern part of the future Park, and after 1871, when trains began to stop at Raynes Park station in the south, did the district begin to attract attention. Until then it seemed an intimidating area which travellers had to pass through on their way to market in Kingston.

114. A map of Cottenham Park, drawn by John Wallace.

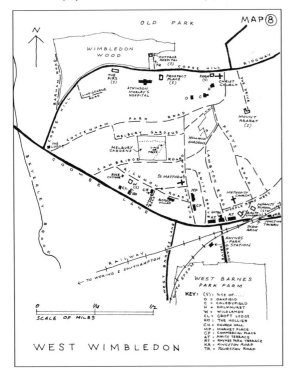

115. Denmark Terrace about 1920, with The King of Denmark on the right and beyond, the shops that served the houses of the Ridgway. The only one that survives today is Jenkins, the newsagent, which then also ran a 'Registry Office for Servants'.

This big market in the centre of the town at-tracted people from a wide area. There they would find goods like salt, butter, fish, wine, timber and cloth.   They could also attend a weekly cattle market, as many local farmers did to buy and sell cows, sheep and horses.   In Victorian times they could also get animal feed there or the latest piece of farm machinery.   Boys walked to Kingston, as Joseph Boulter did from Wimbledon in June 1751, 'to be bound apprentice to Henry Parkhurst, fish-erman'.   A hundred years later young men like Arthur Harmer made regular trips there by train in the 1860s to see their girlfriends.

Before the opening of the railway the route taken by people from the village was along 'Ridge Way Lane' and down Copse Hill to join 'the Lane from Merton' (now Coombe Lane).   Almost certainly it was an ancient highway, but its first mention in any document only comes in the reign of Eliza-beth I.   As late as the 1880s it remained 'a very narrow lane fading away into bluebell woods [about where Drax Avenue is today], full of squir-rels, badgers, nightingales and the harsh cry of the pheasant'.   Every year it was churned up by the hooves of hundreds of Welsh cattle which came to be fattened on meadows near the village before being taken to market in London.

It was near these meadows that the first signs of the growth of Wimbledon appeared. 'Brickfield Cottages' (now Oldfield Road) were built about 1820 by William Eades, a grocer in the High Street, and his example was followed soon afterwards by William Croft, a timber merchant of West Place, who put up twenty-nine more cottages just off the Ridgway at South Place (a road which no longer exists but was behind the King of Denmark). These homes were mainly occupied by agricultural la-bourers and their families.   The real transforma-tion of the Ridgway, however, started in the 1850s with the laying-out of further culs-de-sac such as Sunnyside, Ridgway Place and Hillside, which all went to the crown of the hill and stopped.   The first roads to go all the way down to 'Worple Lane' were Denmark (named after the beerhouse at the top) and Thornton (after the millionaire owner of the land who lived at Cannon Hill House, Merton). Many of the larger houses belonged to prosperous middle-class families like the Fells who moved to Ridgway Place in the early 1880s.   In their home they had a 'very unusual thing, a bathroom', but all the rooms were still lit by candles, though 'there were gas-jets in the hall'.   Behind the house were 'two meadows stretching to St John's church where a flock of sheep used to graze', and the countrified atmosphere was maintained by 'many splendid trees'.

At the top of Denmark Road by the 1860s there

116. Christ Church on 22 April 1905, with the narrow Copse Hill and the hedge of Barns Field to its right and a badly needed drinking trough for horses at the top of Cottenham Park Road to its left.

was also a mini-village. At its centre was a col-lection of model cottages designed by a leading architect, Samuel Teulon, and offered at very moderate rents to 'applicants of good character and cleanly habits'.   Round the corner along the Ridgway was Denmark Terrace, a row of shops including a grocer, a post office and a beer retailer, The King of Denmark, while near by were two important Victorian tradesmen, a blacksmith and 'a mechanical chimney-sweep', who used collaps-ible brushes rather than unfortunate climbing boys.

Teulon also designed three other major build-ings along the Ridgway: the Village Club (1859), Wimbledon School (1860) and Christ Church (1859).   The Club was founded to afford the in-habitants, and more especially the working and middle classes, the opportunities of intellectual and moral improvement through providing a Reading Room for newspapers, a library, and a hall for fortnightly lectures.   The school, on a drive off the Ridgway, was an Army 'crammer', run by 'one of the most conspicuously successful teachers of his day', the Revd John Brackenbury.   It was generally considered to be Teulon's finest work in Wimbledon.

Christ Church, however, is certainly his most important building.   It was only the second church ever built in Wimbledon and the first of a number of 'chapels of ease' to help the Vicar at St Mary's provide services for the ever-growing population. It could seat nearly six hundred people, yet was soon comfortably full with the families of neigh-bouring residents.   These came mainly from the new houses going up in Cottenham Park. The 300-acre estate, owned by the Earl of Cottenham until his death in 1851, had soon been split up.   Forty acres were bought by St George's Hospital for a convalescent home they were planning to build with a legacy from a London hotel owner, Atkinson

118. *Francis Penrose (1817-1903) who lived at Colebyfield, which still survives.*

117. *Thomas Hughes (1822-96), who lived at The Firs. After leaving Wimbledon he became an MP and County Court judge.*

119. *Sir Arthur Holland (c.1845-1928) who lived at Holmhurst, the site now of an old people's home.*

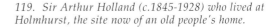

Morley. The rest was sold to London businessmen who formed the Metropolitan and General Freehold Land Society. They laid out roads, named them after local aristocrats like Pepys, Lambton, Durham and Cambridge, divided the land into large plots and hoped a 'high-class residential area' would evolve.

COPSE HILL

Unfortunately for their hopes, the new roads remained empty for years. The only plots to find ready buyers were along the old highway to Kingston, Copse Hill. From the middle 1850s a number of distinguished Victorians built large, if not very beautiful, houses for their families here. Notable among them were Thomas Hughes, one of the leading Christian Socialists who wrote *Tom Brown's Schooldays* for his son Maurice while living at The Firs; Francis Penrose, a distinguished architect and keen archaeologist, one of whose daughters, Emily, was the first woman to get a first-class honours degree in Greats at Oxford; and Sir Arthur Holland, head of a shipping firm, who along with his wife played a leading part in local affairs for nearly fifty years and now has a nearby recreation ground named after him. At

120. Raynes Park Station about 1910 with a tram approaching from Wimbledon. The estate office, railwaymen's cottages and coal merchants' offices have long gone.

first they felt very isolated so far from the village. One of the first residents, Charles Grenside, a London solicitor, always carried a swordstick for the long walk home from Wimbledon station on dark winter evenings. He also kept two revolvers in the house and encouraged his wife to practise shooting at a box in the garden. By the 1870s, however, he would no longer have needed to walk. A special horse omnibus (the precursor of

the present 200 bus) ran 'twice a day morning and evening for businessmen going to and from the station'.

His fears were shared by a voluble Welshman, Bennett Williams. One of the few wealthy men to buy a plot well to the south of Copse Hill, he gave his house on Richmond Road the significant name 'Wildlands'. In 1886 he wrote a very out-spoken letter to the local paper about 'this pretty rural end of the parish'. It was, he claimed, 'a paradise of stray cattle' from nearby farms; they frequently broke into his garden and ate his 'early spring greens'. Burglaries were common as there was rarely a policeman to be seen. The roads were 'almost impassable', while at night 'the feeble glimmer of the wretched oil lamps' made walking hazardous. Perhaps that explains why in the early 1880s there were less than a hundred houses north of Coombe Lane, mostly small working-class homes along Richmond Road and Amity Grove, served by shops on Durham Road and opposite the new Raynes Park station.   The only person who seems to have been hopeful of the district's future was J.E. Knox, owner of one of the first houses in Coombe Lane. In 1881 he founded the Cottenham Park Institute at a Hall he built in Avenue Road 'for the mental and moral improve-ment of the residents'. There they could find

121. The bottom of Durham Road about 1920. The shops, including Jeffreys the fishmonger, are hidden behind the belt of trees on the right. St Matthew's church, opened in 1910, is as yet without its nave and bell towers.

123. Coombe Lane near the junction with Cambridge Road about 1920. The Edwardian houses on the right mostly survive. Behind the drainage ditch and trees on the left are the fields of Hoppingwood Farm, New Malden. They were not developed until the late 1920s.

122. Cottenham Park Road, just beyond the junction with Durham Road, in the 1920s.

reading and smoking rooms, as well as enjoy concerts and talks for a very reasonable subscription. The Institute was succeeded in 1914 by the West Wimbledon Society which still regularly meets in the same Hall.

By 1914 Knox's hope had been justified and Cottenham Park was no longer 'isolated and neglected'. First the extension of Worple Road and then in 1907 the arrival of trams from Kingston made the district of much greater interest to young families wanting to settle in Wimbledon. They soon had plenty of homes to choose from – small, relatively cheap ones in Durham, Lambton and Pepys Roads, as well as a series of new Roads between Lambton and Pepys (all with Cornish names given by the builder, William Peters, a Cornishman); 'maisonettes' with the recently introduced electric light and running hot and cold water, put up by Mr McNeil round the Cambridge –Durham crossroads; and 'highly decorative' Edwardian semis in Dunmore and Stanton Roads on the old Devas estate. Yet the country had still not completely disappeared. Above Dunmore Road were fields used for the local Flower Show, while down Cottenham Park Road it was hard to imagine a town was anywhere near, especially round the allotments, the earliest and largest in Wimbledon, opened in 1893 and soon flourishing on centuries of leaf mould from Pettiward Wood that once covered the area.

The fields and woods owned by the Drax family north of Copse Hill was the area of Wimbledon that remained undeveloped longest. In 1924 Captain (later Admiral) the Hon. Reginald Ranfurly Plunkett-Ernle-Erle-Drax RN, a distinguished

sailor who fought at Jutland, and was also an expert on solar heating, decided to sell the land for building. Roads were laid out and named after ships on which he had served or after family estates. Alfred Styles, 'Contractor and Estate Developer', built numerous 'high-class residences', fitted with central heating and provided with a recent addition to local houses, a garage. They were said to be 'comfortable, labour-saving homes', planned 'to take full advantage of the sun and views'. At the same time Copse Hill was widened to take an increased volume of traffic, inevitable after the Kingston By-Pass was opened in 1927 by the Prime Minister, Stanley Baldwin. In its turn that led to the development of the southern part of Copse Hill from Barham Road (originally the drive to Warren Farm) down to Coombe Lane. Here in 1933 the countryside made a final farewell to Wimbledon when the Bath and West Show was held in fields soon to be covered by the houses of Beverley and Holland Avenues.

TOYNBEE ROAD

Meanwhile, an alternative route to Kingston from 'New Wimbledon' had been opened up. For centuries 'Lower Worple' had simply led to fields and to a right of way to Merton Hall Farm on Kingston Road. In the 1870s this cart track was renamed Dundonald Road when small roads with working-class houses were laid out near the railway goods yard. In 1882 the large Merton Hall estate just to the south was sold as 'ripe for immediate building'. Large houses began to go up along Merton Hall Road. There was still, however, no way through to Lower Downs Road (another old right of way) since David Thomson, a nurseryman who had just lost most of his land on

Wimbledon Hill, had leased the land for his plants and fruit trees.   Then, just after the First World War, the Council, under pressure from Lloyd George's government to provide more working-class homes, compulsorily purchased the Nurs-.ery.   Their experts decided to visit a Rowntree Trust garden suburb near York and came back inspired to try a similar experiment here.   In the early 1920s the houses they built for renting on very moderate terms were given large gardens and were well set back from tree-lined roads (named Toynbee after the local Victorian philanthropist, Burstow after a village near Gatwick once linked to Wimbledon and Dennis Park Crescent after the Borough Surveyor's son).   The estate that then grew up has been described as 'an impressive advance on what had previously been provided for working people in Wimbledon'.   Seventy-five years later it still keeps its special character.

124. Cottenham Park from the air in 1919. In the foreground are Cambridge, Richmond, Durham, Lambton and Pepys Roads, with wartime allotments on the far right, where Devas and Hunter Roads were to be built. In the centre is Cottenham Park Road and above it the estates of Lindisfarne House (on the left), Atkinson Morley's Hospital (in the middle) and the houses along Copse Hill (to the right). At the top, beyond Wimbledon Wood and the fairways of the Royal Wimbledon golf course, are the huts of the First World War Army Camp, still on the Common.

125. *Queen Victoria listening to an address of welcome at the first NRA meeting on the Common, 2 July 1860. To the left fly the flags of all the nations taking part.*

Victoria, the Kaiser and 'A Day ever to be remembered'

QUEEN VICTORIA AT THE N.R.A.

On 28 January 1861, just outside the Cottenham Park estate, there was a serious railway accident. An express from Waterloo plunged down the steep embankment near the junction with the line to Epsom (where Raynes Park Station is today). A number of passengers were injured, but only one was killed. Tragically he was the Queen's Doctor, William Baly, a man in his late forties and an expert on dysentery and cholera. In just two years he had gained both Victoria's and Albert's 'entire confidence'. His loss was serious, as later that year the overworked Prince caught typhoid, but could not be persuaded to rest till too late. His death early in December might have been prevented if the trusted and competent Dr Baly had been on hand. If so, the Queen would not have become a recluse, and 'the widow of Windsor'.

A year earlier in much happier circumstances Victoria and her husband had paid their only joint visit to Wimbledon. They had been invited to inaugurate the first meeting of the National Rifle Association on the Common. The NRA had been formed in 1859 to improve the marksmanship of Britain's home defence force, the Volunteers, in the face of an imagined threat of French invasion. They had been offered the use of the Common by the 5th Earl Spencer, still lord of the manor even though his father had sold Wimbledon Park. The local Volunteers, among them H.C. Forde, a telegraph engineer living in Ridgway Place, were commissioned to set up a line of butts for shooting

126. *Shooting at an NRA meeting about 1870.*
Spectators and off-duty competitors are watching the
marksmen from behind a wooden barrier.

127. *Queensmere crowded with holiday-makers about*
1910.

practice, but they were held up by weeks of rain
and only just finished the work in time.

Monday, 2 July 1860 was fortunately fine. The
Queen with Prince Albert, the young Edward Prince
of Wales and several princesses drove in procession through Wimbledon Park and along Church
Road. In the High Street, lined by Forde and the
Volunteers, they passed under a triumphal arch
and then along Parkside to near the Windmill
where the Queen alighted. She was greeted by
the Prime Minister, Lord Palmerston, the Secretary of State for War, Sidney Herbert, the head of
the NRA, Lord Elcho, Earl Spencer and an assem-
bly of soldiers from many nations, as well as a
large crowd of spectators. Sidney Herbert made
an address of welcome and then led her to a special
pavilion where Joseph Whitworth had set up one
of his new rifles in a special mechanical rest,
sighted on a target in the Queen's Butt four hundred

128. *The Kaiser reviewing the London Rifle Brigade, 11*
July 1891. It was the last great military review on the
Common.

yards away. The Queen pulled a red silken cord and from the side of the target there soon fluttered a red and white flag to show that her shot had hit within a quarter of an inch of the bull's eye.

The fortnight's shooting competition she thus inaugurated continued every summer until 1889. It drew large crowds and became one of the chief features of the London season. 'Going to Wimbledon' for Victorians meant for many thousands a long walk or carriage drive to the Common, where, it was said, 'the shooting is not particularly interesting, but the refreshment department supplies everything a visitor can reasonably require', and where parties round the competitors' tents went on long into the night. In the end the rifles became too powerful and the meetings had to be moved to Bisley.

In June 1887, three years before that happened, the Queen celebrated her Golden Jubilee. Wimbledon marked the occasion by creating a new lake on the Common in her honour. Workmen dammed a stream running through a meadow beside the Windmill (once the scene of duels) and so made The Queen's Mere. Ten years later the Queen's Diamond Jubilee was also celebrated on the Common. While many adults attended church services and two hundred 'Old Folks' were given a special dinner at the Drill Hall in St George's Road, masses of children were entertained with swings and roundabouts, coconut shies and Punch and Judy shows. At nightfall came the climax. With Rushmere illuminated with hundreds of Chinese lanterns, a huge bonfire was lit and myriads of fireworks were set off, ending with a massive set piece – a portrait of the Queen.

THE KAISER ON THE COMMON

11 July 1891 was another notable day in the history of the Common: a review of 22,000 soldiers, Regulars and Volunteers, on an afternoon of 'blazing sun' by Kaiser Wilhelm II. The German Emperor had come to England on his first State visit after taking control from his great Chancellor, Count Bismarck. Welcomed by *The Times* as 'a youthful ruler whom Englishmen admire for his self-reliance and ardent patriotism', he had first visited his grandmother, Queen Victoria, at Windsor Castle and had also been received by the City of London. But for him the highlight of the visit was the review. For this 6,000 Regulars had marched up from Aldershot, while 16,000 Volunteers in their scarlet uniforms had arrived at the special station below St George's Road before assembling on the Common. There they were drawn up in a long line – the infantry below the Windmill, the gunners and cavalry nearer to Rushmere.

At three o'clock the Emperor's train drew in to Wimbledon Station. He was greeted by a salvo of guns and by a triumphal arch across the bridge and he then rode up the Hill at the head of a long line of 'brilliantly uniformed horsemen', including his cousins, the Prince of Wales and Arthur Duke of Connaught, the Commander-in-Chief. But he outshone them all in his dazzling white uniform and gilt helmet with a silver German eagle on top. Crowds three or four deep lined the pavements, while flags and bunting hung across the road. On the Common the crowds were even bigger, with peers, MPs and diplomats in a special stand just behind the reviewing base off Parkside. After the German national anthem had been played, the Kaiser cantered down the long line of soldiers to review them. He then took the salute as first the infantry marched past, followed by the gunners. Finally the cavalry – the Blues and Dragoon Guards – charged, covering everyone with clouds of dust. The Kaiser was most impressed and later wrote to one of the royal Dukes: 'I still remember with unalloyed pleasure the magnificent sight on Wimbledon Common. It was the greatest treat you could have imagined for me and splendidly done'.

It was 'a day ever to be remembered in the annals of Wimbledon', according to the printer Edwin Trim, in the introduction to one of his local Directories. Since 1914, however, it has very understandably been forgotten, except by historians. Far more worthy of memory are six other days in the last thirty years of Queen Victoria's reign: 16 August 1871 (the signing of the Wimbledon and Putney Commons Act), 9 July 1877 (the start of the first All-England Lawn Tennis Championships), 9 March 1887 (the opening of the Public Library), 3 June 1889 (the arrival of the first District Railway engine at Wimbledon Station), 13 May 1891 (the opening of the Worple Road Extension), and 17 July 1899 (the start of the Electricity Generating Station at Durnsford Road). The Tennis Championships and Worple Road Extension have already been dealt with, but the other four events are just as important. All were major landmarks in the history of Wimbledon.

SAVING THE COMMONS

All four too aroused controversy, but the most bitter was that over the future of the Common. In 1864 Earl Spencer, having seen its sad state at close quarters as an NRA competitor, decided to try and improve matters. He introduced a Bill in the House of Lords to enclose most of Wimbledon Common as a public park, 'for the enjoyment and

129. *John, 5th Earl Spencer (1835-1910), in his garter robes for the coronation of Edward VII in 1902. The page is his young nephew, later the 7th Earl (1892-1975).*

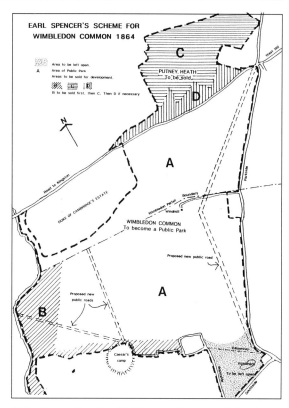

130. *A map showing Earl Spencer's proposals for the improvement of the common in 1864, drawn by Paul Bowness.*

recreation of the inhabitants'. To pay for a new wall and a fence round it and for new roads across it, he proposed to sell Putney Heath for development. Many people felt that his scheme was both sensible and generous, but the wealthy, professional residents of the new houses along Parkside (men like William Williams, a solicitor, and Joseph Toynbee) strongly disagreed. They wanted 'an untamed Common' and formed the Commons Preservation Committee to preserve it 'unenclosed for the benefit of the neighbourhood and the public'. To secure their object they raised nearly £10,000 and fought a long legal battle in the Court of Chancery.

In the end the Earl decided there was little point in carrying on the struggle as there was now a growing body of opinion all over the country against the enclosure of Commons. So he agreed to a compromise: in return for a yearly payment of £1,200 (his average annual income from the Commons), he would give 'his estate and interest' in them to a body of Conservators whose duty was 'to keep the Commons open, unenclosed and unbuilt on' and to preserve them 'for the purpose of exercise and recreation'. The Wimbledon and Putney Commons Act received the royal assent on 16 August 1871. A fortnight later the conservators under the chairmanship of Sir Henry Peek MP held their first meeting. Ever since, the Commons they control have given untold pleasure to generations of Wimbledonians.

THE FIRST LIBRARY

The Free Public Library has given equal delight to many thousands of readers over the past century. Yet the proposal to set one up in Wimbledon led to a long and noisy debate. The idea was first put forward in 1880 by James Van Sommer, a solicitor and temperance campaigner, and Norman Bazalgette, son of the great engineer. They argued that there was an urgent need to make books available to working people who could not afford the cost of joining one of the subscription libraries. But they met strong opposition, espe-

131. Henry Bull, Wimbledon's Chief Librarian, 1896-1935. The photograph was taken in the Reference Library, shortly after it opened in 1903.

cially from Colonel Cole, Chairman of the Local Board, who claimed that it was wrong to spend public money on books and that the Board's duty was to keep the rates down. A poll of ratepayers narrowly backed the Colonel, but the Library supporters refused to give up. In 1886 the Board, under a new Chairman, John Townsend, approved the idea and bought half David Thomson's Nursery on Wimbledon Hill from the Church Commissioners as its site. They employed Messrs Potts, Sulman and Hennings to design the Library, one of the more distinguished Victorian buildings in Wimbledon – especially as it then had trees, railings and a privet hedge in front.

The formal opening on 9 March 1887 was performed by Sir John Lubbock MP (later Lord Avebury), a leading campaigner for free libraries. His 'scholarly address' was full of quotations from Greek and other authors, and was followed by four other speakers, including two MPs and the Board Chairman. The ceremony was graced by the Vicar of Wimbledon who read prayers and by a Volunteer Guard of Honour, and ended with the National Anthem. At first, however, only the

Reading Room for newspapers (where the Issue Desk is today) was ready. The Lending and Reference Libraries opened nine months later when there were enough books to fill the shelves. By then the success of the Library was assured with over a twelfth of the adult population already members. By the turn of the century new lending and reference sections were needed. They were added to the rear of the original Library and were designed by Robert Thomson, the architect son of the displaced nurseryman.

EXTENDING THE DISTRICT LINE

At the same time as the dispute raged over the Library, an equally bitter controversy broke out over future routes for the District Railway. In 1880 its trains from West London reached Putney Bridge and an extension of the line was then proposed to Guildford via Kingston, crossing the Common. It was strongly opposed by the South-Western Railway and by the Commons Conservators led by Sir Henry Peek, supported by leading residents. In the end a compromise was reached. The line across the Common was abandoned and the South-Western Railway took over the extension from Putney Bridge, re-routeing it via Southfields and Wimbledon Park to Wimbledon, where a new terminus would be built, north of the present station. The line would be owned by the South-Western Railway, but the trains would be operated by the District.

On 3 June 1889 the first engine with its brown carriages pulled into the new Wimbledon Station. It started what was claimed to be a half-hourly service, 'a quick and cheap route to London' (though on Sundays there were no trains during the hours of divine service). Whether this claim

132. A District Railway steam engine pulling its carriages from Wimbledon Park to Wimbledon Station, just before the line was electrified in 1905.

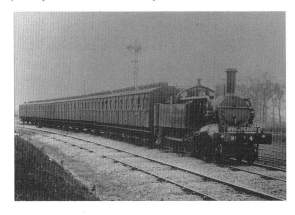

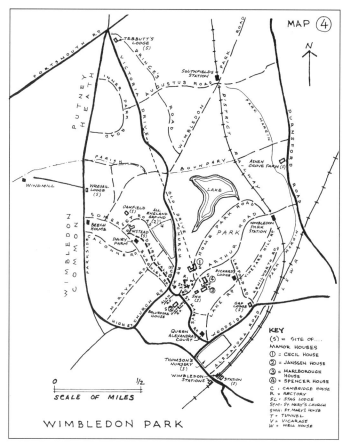

133. A map of Wimbledon Park, drawn by John Wallace.

was justified before the line was electrified in 1905 (ten years before the main line to Waterloo) is a matter of debate, but the start of a relatively frequent service to London transformed Wimbledon Park. Till then Mr Beaumont's attempt to develop the southern half of his estate round Arthur and Lake Roads had held fire. From 1889, however, there was dramatic change. First, houses went up near the District terminus – along Woodside, Vineyard Hill and Kenilworth Avenue. After 1905 development shifted to the area round Wimbledon Park station, as a result of Henry Penfold, a property developer, and George Ryan, a builder and estate agent, opening an office in Arthur Road. They put up rows of villas in the nearby roads along the railway, which have come to be known as 'The Grid'. Their first hundred houses 'on this charming estate' were seemingly 'offered For Nothing' – in fact at a special discount. The bait worked and attracted the sort of people Penfold especially wished to house – superior working-class families whose fathers worked as clerks,

134. Woodside Parade, Leopold Road, about 1910.

salesmen, policemen or chauffeurs. They were provided with well-built homes, where bathrooms were now standard features. They thus created one of the most cohesive districts in Wimbledon, with probably the earliest Residents' Association.

THE NEW POWER STATION

The final day 'ever to be remembered' in Queen Victoria's reign came just two years before her death. On 17 July 1899 electricity was first generated at a new Power Station in Durnsford Road, built to the designs of Arthur Preece. His father, Sir William, owner of Gothic Lodge near the Crooked Billet and said to be 'the best known engineer in Britain', had long campaigned for Wimbledon's streets to be lit by electricity. His ideas were turned down by the Local Board who felt electricity was still unreliable and that gas or oil was preferable. The gas was provided from works near the Wandle, but the Company refused to lay mains in the new roads being laid out in 1880. So the Board decided to light the streets with oil lamps. Four years later Preece was asked by the Corporation of London to demonstrate the effectiveness of electric light. He chose the High Street, Wimbledon, as the ideal place to do it and for three months had 76 lamps suspended over the road. The experiment was pronounced a great success, but the Board (supported by the Ratepayers' Association) was still not convinced. It was left to Preece's son to win over the members of the Urban District Council (which had taken over from the Board in 1895) and persuade them to support a Private Bill in Parliament allowing them to run an electricity station.

Once electric light was available in Wimbledon, an increasing number of old homes were converted from oil or gas, while all new houses were wired for electricity. But the biggest change came in the streets. William Stoakley, editor of *The Wimbledon News* for over forty years, was asked in 1934 which were the biggest changes he had seen in the borough. He replied that among the most dramatic was the transformation in the streets when the dim oil lamps were replaced with bright electric lights. All who experienced the blackout in the Second World War will appreciate what he meant.

136. The Electricity Power Station, Durnsford Road, about 1914. It was pulled down in 1965.

135. The bottom of Arthur Road, just before the First World War, with Wimbledon Park Station behind the children on the left and Ryan and Penfold's office on the right.

Ten Victorian Residents

137. *(Above) Sir Joseph Bazalgette (1819-1891) and his wife. As Chief Engineer to the Metropolitan Board of Works, he was responsible for constructing London's sewers, the Thames Embankment and Battersea and Putney Bridges. In 1873 he settled at St Mary's House, Arthur Road, opposite the parish church. There he was able to relax, read and look after his garden.*

138 *(Top right) Sir Francis Fox (1844-1927). Another great engineer, he designed the first tunnel under the Mersey, the Great Central Railway and the first London Tube. His greatest achievement (together with Sir Thomas Jackson and a brave diver) was to save Winchester Cathedral from collapse. In 1894 he settled at Alyn Bank, The Downs (later St Theresa's Hospital) and lived there until his death.*

139 *(Right) Sir Charles Tyrrell Giles (1850-1940). He grew up in Wimbledon and after his marriage settled at Copse Hill House (the site of Cottenham Drive). He was a local JP and a Commons Conservator from 1890. His great achievement was to save the Royal Wimbledon golf course from development in the 1930s.*

142. *Sir Henry Peek (1825-1898). Partner in a firm of colonial merchants, he bought Wimbledon House Parkside in 1854. As MP for East Surrey he later played an important part in securing the passing of the Commons Act in 1871.*

140. *Sir Thomas Jackson (1835-1924). A distinguished architect, he saved Eagle House from development in 1886 and restored it as a home. He designed several buildings in Wimbledon, notably St John's church, as well as the War Memorial.*

141. *Sir Norman Lockyer (1836-1920). A distinguished astronomer, he settled at 14 Hillside, off the Ridgway, in 1858, when only a clerk at the War Office. When first interested in astronomy he installed a telescope in his garden. He moved to Hampstead in 1865, where he became famous as the discoverer of helium.*

143. *Sir William Preece (1834-1913). The Chief Engineer at the Post Office, he bought Gothic Lodge in 1874 and made it the centre for many experiments, especially in electricity. His was the first house in the London area to have electric light, an electric kettle and a telephone. He ws very friendly with Marconi and together in his garden they set up a transmitter for the newly-invented wireless telegraph.*

144. *(Above) William Stead (1849-1912). A leading Victorian journalist, he bought Cambridge House, Church Road, opposite the Rectory, for his wife and six children in 1880. He was famous for exposing 'criminal vice' in England and for strongly opposing the Boer War. He lost his life on the Titanic.*

145. *(Top right) Joseph Toynbee (1815-1866). A pioneering ear, nose and throat specialist, he moved in 1854 with his large family to Beecholme, one of the mansions recently built on Parkside. He played a leading role in founding the Village Club and would have started a museum had he not died suddenly.*

146. *(Bottom right) William Williams (1806-80), a solicitor who came to live in another of the new houses along Parkside. He was an important member of the Wimbledon and Putney Commons Defence Committee and helped to secure the passing of the 1871 Act. He was therefore chosen as one of the first Conservators.*

147. Charter Day, 26 July 1905. Mr Butterworth reads the Charter from the temporary balcony in front of the Town Hall, with the white-bearded Mayor behind him. The dignitaries sit in the foreground behind the guard of honour.

The Edwardian Borough

CHARTER DAY

Edwin Trim had described the Kaiser's visit in 1891 as 'a day ever to be remembered in the annals of Wimbledon'. Early in the reign of Edward VII, *The Wimbledon News* echoed this idea, declaring that 26 July 1905 was 'a day never to be forgotten by those who took part'. The event was Charter Day, the celebration of Wimbledon's achievement in becoming a borough and gaining its own Mayor. All who took part are almost certainly now dead and the Day, like the Kaiser's visit, has been forgotten except by historians. The Charter itself, which was meant to last for generations was overridden only sixty years later when Wimbledon became part of a new London borough.

Yet in 1905 the securing of a Charter seemed a great triumph. It was an official acknowledgement of Wimbledon's success in transforming itself from the 'beautiful and highly genteel village' of the 1850s into 'much more than a London suburb'. The demand for a Charter had started soon after the Urban District Council had taken over from the Local Board in 1895. Leading councillors such as Charles Tyrrell Giles (of Copse Hill House, a JP and Chairman of the Conservators) and Colonel Thomas Mitchell (a notable athlete and director of a tapestry firm who lived at Cannizaro) argued that Wimbledon was entitled to the greater dignity of a Borough. Since 1885 it had returned its own Member of Parliament and two years later it had nearly been chosen as the headquarters of the new Surrey County Council rather than Kingston. Many ordinary ratepayers however, felt that the extra powers given to a Borough Council would mean 'freer scope for extravagance' and at a lively public meeting in Worple Hall voted decisively against it. But the councillors, strongly supported by local tradesmen, refused to give up. They canvassed each district in turn and found in every one, except in Cottenham Park, a majority in their favour. In April 1904, with this backing and a petition with over 6,000 signatures, they formally applied to the Privy Council for the right to become a borough. A year later, the request was granted and the Charter received the royal assent.

On 26 July 1905 in 'glorious summer weather' the first Mayor, Alderman Hamshaw, and the new Town Clerk, Mr Butterworth, brought the document in its red case from Westminster. At the borough boundary with Merton they were greeted

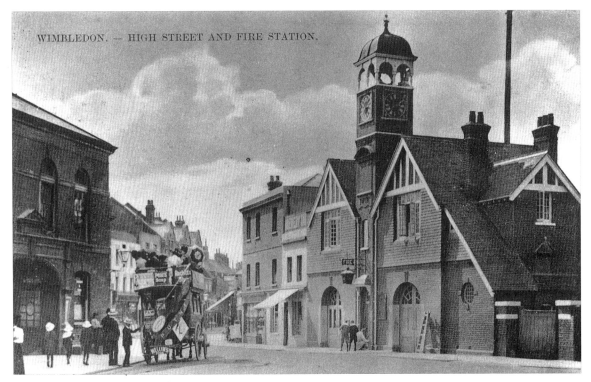

WIMBLEDON. — HIGH STREET AND FIRE STATION.

148. The Fire Station in the High Street opposite the Dog and Fox. It had only a short life, from 1890 to 1907.

by crowds which grew as they drove up the Broadway in a procession of over forty carriages. At the gaily decorated Town Hall they went out onto a temporary balcony where Mr Butterworth read the Charter to the many dignitaries seated behind the guard of honour from the Surrey Yeomanry, while the Mayor in his speech declared that this was 'the most important event in the history of our town'. They then processed up the Hill to King's College Hall where there was a lavish lunch, followed by more speeches. Meanwhile, across Southside the Common was alive with schoolchildren enjoying swings and roundabouts and watching a two mile long procession of decorated tradesmen's carts. At nightfall there was a torchlit procession, followed by the traditional bonfire and fireworks. 'Never yet was a Borough launched under happier auspices' was the verdict of the renamed *Wimbledon Boro' News*.

In the few years before 1914 the Mayor, eight aldermen and 24 councillors did partly justify these high hopes. They produced a more efficient Fire Brigade under Captain Butler. He insisted that a majority of his firemen should be paid, full-time employees and that they must aim to be far

149. The new Fire Station in Queens Road just after its opening in 1904, with one of the steam fire-engines pulled by two fine greys, and the Brigade's greyhound mascot which used to run in front of the engine.

quicker in reaching a fire. He even trained the greys who pulled the engines to slip their heads into the harness as soon as the alarm rang, but in 1913, in the interests of greater efficiency, sadly replaced them with motors.

Public health was also greatly improved, thanks to the work of two Council officials – the Medical Officer of Health, Evelyn Pocklington, and the Borough Surveyor, Charles Cooper. Dr Pocklington, the first to hold the job, carried on an untiring campaign to control serious epidemics, especially among children. By the time he retired in 1909 (after 33 years) he could report a steady decrease in deaths from diphtheria and scarlet fever, and a general death-rate in the borough just over half the national average. Cooper (who held his post nearly as long, from 1890 to 1918) helped by improving the water supply, the treatment of sewage and the collection and disposal of house refuse. He thus helped to justify the *Town Guide*, when it claimed that 'the town is thoroughly up to date in all those matters which go to make a desirable place of residence, having a splendid water supply, perfect sanitation, and

well laid-out streets'.

It also acquired in 1912 its first general hospitals: the Wimbledon Hospital, Copse Hill, which replaced the tiny cottage hospital, and the Nelson Hospital, Kingston Road, founded 'to serve Wimbledon, Merton and District'. The Nelson was largely the work of a young doctor, Frank Deas, helped by men like Colonel Mitchell and Charles Tyrrell Giles. He first set up a small cottage hospital in Merton Road and then, after the Trafalgar Centenary celebrations in 1905 had raised over £3,000, decided to found an up-to-date Nelson Memorial Hospital. It took seven years to carry out and has since won the gratitude of innumerable patients.

The Council did not, however, gain any gratitude from many families in South Wimbledon. They were accused of doing little to help the unemployed, especially during the winter of 1909 when bad weather and a serious slump in trade reduced some to near destitution. Discontent was also voiced by another group who felt ignored by those in power – the Women's Social and Political Union who demanded 'Votes for Women'. A

150. A suffragette meeting on the Common in 1913, addressed by Mrs Rose Lamartine Yates.

Wimbledon Branch with offices and a shop in Victoria Crescent was formed in 1908. From the start it was one of the most militant branches in the London area and produced notable speakers like Rose Lamartine Yates of Dorset Hall, Kingston Road, and Mrs Begbie who lived on the Ridgway. Every Sunday afternoon they addressed suffragette meetings on the Common, often under police protection. Afterwards Mrs Begbie sometimes had to be escorted home. In 1912 both ladies were imprisoned for a short time, yet on release organised 'Women's Sunday', a great open-air demonstration on the Common with over 20,000 supporters from all over London. They did not win the vote until after the First World War, but prepared the way for the far greater part women were to play in national life during that War.

TRAMS, CYCLES AND CARS

Apart from Charter Day, there were three other occasions 'never to be forgotten' by Edwardian citizens of Wimbledon. The first was the arrival of the trams on 2 May 1907, in the face of a lot of controversy. A number of people objected to the extra noise they would cause on top of that of carts and carriages with their iron-bound wheels. Cyclists naturally feared accidents through their tyres getting stuck in the tramlines. Shopkeepers opposite Elys (including Russell's, the famous photographers) objected to the cutting of their premises in half to fit in a double track for the trams, while householders in Worple Road were naturally unhappy to lose their front gardens. But above all, many, especially in 'North Wimbledon', feared that trams would bring thousands of 'working men' to the Borough, as under a law of 1844 all machines running on wheels had to provide cheap early fares. The five-year delay in starting the service also gave cartoonists a field day. Nonetheless the majority seem to have welcomed the trams. Seventy years later an elderly lady still vividly remembered the first one passing her school near the Skew Arch in Raynes Park and being taken outside with her class to watch an historic event. Passengers began to use the tram instead of the train: the service was cheaper and more regular. The railway in fact did not recover until its suburban lines were electrified in 1915.

151. The arrival of the first tram at Elys Corner in August 1906. It was only a trial, watched by Board of Trade inspectors. The service began in the following year, but the shops on the Pavement (to the right), as well as Elys (opposite) had already been forced to adjust their fronts to allow room for twin tracks.

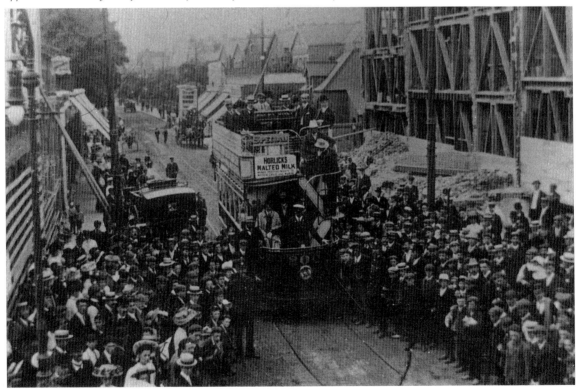

Meantime, despite the tram tracks, 'a bicycling epidemic' had hit Wimbledon. The 'ordinary' or pennyfarthing had been replaced in the late 1880s by the 'safety bicycle' with its Dunlop pneumatic tyres. Cycle clubs, like the Mid-Surrey Cyclists, had gone touring all round the Surrey countryside. With the men for the first time went their wives or girlfriends, liberated from their hooped skirts and wearing 'stiff collars, blouses with big sleeves and hard little straw hats'. But around 1904, even before the trams appeared, the roads had become less safe, as a brief item in *The Wimbledon News* indicated: 'A car hit a bicycle near the Grove and threw the cyclist off'. The motor had begun to make its presence felt.

When the first car was seen in Wimbledon is uncertain. It was probably about 1900 and the earliest motorist Señor Ricardo Jimenez, the London manager of a Spanish firm, who lived at Lindisfarne House, Copse Hill. Certainly by 1904 cars were regularly in the news. Two collided in Worple Road; a lady in one was thrown out and badly bruised her shoulder. A small boy was knocked down by 'a motor driven by William Way'; he suffered a slight head wound. Above all J.M. Boustead of Westfield, Parkside, was fined two pounds for 'furious motor driving' – at 25 mph on the Portsmouth Road, Surbiton, instead of observing the limit of 20 mph. By 1914 there were seventeen garages in the borough. Among

153. The top of the Broadway just before the First World War, with a solitary car approaching the bridge.

them was The Wimbledon Horse, Carriage and Motor Company run by Henry Dormer from his home at The Hermitage, West Place. Ten years earlier he had simply run a 'Livery and Bait Stables; Broughams and Carriages for hire'. Now he advertised 'Omnibuses for families; Luggage to any of the Metropolitan Stations'. The Wimbledon Motor Works, founded in 1904 by the Oates brothers with just one mechanic, was also flourishing, as were taxi firms, while motor buses with their solid rubber tyres had now taken over from horses.

152. T.H. Proctor, 'Contractor to the Wimbledon Borough Council'. In fact, a scrap dealer of North Road (off Haydons Road), photographed with his family about 1910.

154. *'Jack' in action up Wimbledon Hill, probably in the 1920s.*

155. *The bottom of Hill Road seen from the bridge about 1912, just after the introduction of motor buses.*

156. *The top of the Hill about 1905, with a warning to motorists going down.*

157. *The junction of the Hill, the Ridgway and the High Street in 1910, with the Toynbee Fountain now on the pavement and just beyond, a watering cart filling up from a pump. The shops on the left had all been built by the 1870s; those on the right with the fine Bank building only went up after the Belvedere estate was developed about 1900.*

Yet in 1914 most transport was still horse-drawn. The most notable were the carts that used to take the heavy loads of coal from the yard at Wimbledon Station. The horses that dragged the loads, often two tons or more, up Wimbledon Hill aroused the concern of Miss Ethel Crickmay, daughter of a local councillor. Supported by the Dumb Friends' League and helped by a public subscription raised through an appeal in *The Boro' News*, she was able to station a horse, always known as Jack, near the bottom of the Hill. He started work on 25 May 1908, acting as a trace horse attached by the side or in the front of the original horse. Those that needed his help were charged only a small fee, but 'to the poor and all small owners' his services were free. Other horses pulling loads were not forgotten. At the top of Wimbledon and Copse Hills were horse-troughs placed there by the Metropolitan Cattle-Trough and Drinking Fountains Association. Near by were special pumps with nozzles for filling the water-carts used every summer for damping the very dusty gravel roads, which were yet to be covered with tarmac.

THEATRE, CINEMAS AND CONCERTS

A further 'day never to be forgotten' was 26 December 1910, when Wimbledon's 'Theatre Royal' opened with a pantomime *Jack and Jill*. Seventy years later it was still remembered by Patrick Fawcett. He recalled 'the pillared entrance hall, the ceiling of the auditorium, the crimson carpets and seats, the rich grandeur of it all'. It was the creation of 'a man of vision', J.L. Mulholland, the owner and manager, who believed that a theatre was vital to the life of a town. His policy was to put on plays and shows in Wimbledon before they opened in the West End. So before the First World War he engaged F.R. Benson to take the lead in *Hamlet* and Martin-Harvey in *The Tale of Two Cities*, while the D'Oyly Carte Opera company performed *Iolanthe*.

By then the Theatre was already facing competition from the cinema. The first in Wimbledon, 'The Electric Theatre' (which soon became 'The Queen's Picture Theatre') operating in the Worple Hall opposite Elys, opened in 1909. It drew large crowds the following year with film of the King's funeral, but was soon faced by a rival. In October 1910 (just before the Theatre opened) The King's Palace in the Broadway was launched as a 'luxurious' place of entertainment with four hundred tip-up seats, programmes changed twice a week and free teas and light refreshments for those in

158. *The Queen's Cinema, Worple Road about 1910. It was destroyed by fire in April 1930.*

159. *The Theatre in the Broadway, about 1922. When opened in 1910, it had one of the largest stages in the country, with lights that ran off its own power supply. Despite many crises, it still flourishes.*

160. *The Elite Cinema in the Broadway opened in 1920. It was notable for its decor, but was pulled down in the 1970s*

the shilling or two shilling seats. The Queen's promptly retorted with the claim that it was 'cool in the summer, warm in winter', changed programmes daily, and provided a regular newsreel. The battle for audiences had begun.

For music lovers, concerts had begun in the 1880s with the foundation of the Wimbledon Choral Society. But the real creator of a local orchestra was a German music teacher, Herr Gustav Mächtig, who had come to Wimbledon as a young man in 1881. Fourteen years later he gave his first concert with the Wimbledon Amateur Orchestra, composed mostly of ladies. Its programmes were varied – single movements from symphonies and concertos, mixed with vocal and instrumental solos. The concerts in local halls were very popular and Herr Mächtig, 'a vigorous conductor and real showman', became a well-known personality. Ill-health forced him to give up the concerts in 1913 and his work has since been almost forgotten.

SPORT

Far better remembered are Wimbledon's sports clubs. Several have already celebrated their centenary, notably the Cricket Club (1854), the Royal Wimbledon Golf Club (1865) and the Men's (1883) and Ladies' (1889) Hockey Clubs. In 1908 when the Royal Wimbledon left the Common for a new course on land once part of Warren Farm, their old course was taken over by the Wimbledon Common Golf Club, famous for their red jackets. Three years later a football team composed of ex-pupils of the Old Central School, Camp Road, who had been playing matches on the Common since 1889, formed themselves into the Wimbledon Football Club and moved to a ground off Worple Road. They played in a variety of South London Leagues and won a Charity Cup, but like their present-day successors they had ground trouble and even seem to have been in danger of suspension, when in 1910 they took over an old refuse dump in Plough Lane and laid out a pitch with stands which remained their home until the 1990s.

23 MORE CHURCHES

The final memorable day before the start of the First World War was certainly the most unusual. It was Thursday, 27 March 1913, the occasion of the funeral of a priest, Fr William Kerr SJ. Twenty-six years earlier, when he and a fellow Jesuit had taken lodgings in Cranbrook Road to serve the new church of the Sacred Heart on Edge Hill, they had been greeted by a letter in the local paper from a member of the Protestant Reformation Society attacking the arrival of 'unwelcome strangers who are trying to settle in our town'. Fr Kerr overcame such prejudice by his help for families in distress and his care for the sick and the poor especially in South Wimbledon. By the time of his death he

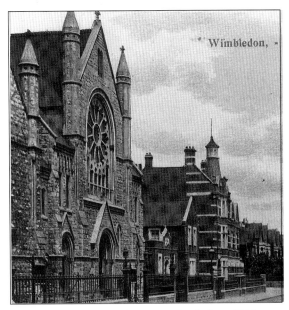

161. *The Baptist Church, Queens Road about 1910. Beyond are the Magistrates' courts and the Fire Station.*

162. *The Presbyterian church in Mansel Road, about 1912. It was opened in 1891 and is now a United Reformed church. Beyond is the High School for Girls, founded in 1880.*

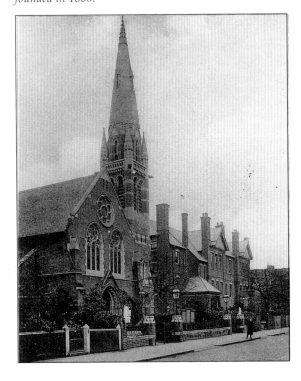

163. The Methodist church and Bond Memorial Hall, Raynes Park, in 1928. The church was opened in 1914, the second Methodist building along Worple Road. The Hall was named after William Bond, one of the founders of Methodism in Cottenham Park.

164. The Roman Catholic church of the Sacred Heart, Edge Hill, in the 1930s before wartime bombing knocked the pinnacles off the buttresses at the east end. It was opened in 1887.

165. The Roman Catholic chapel, Barkby Close, Cottenham Park Road, about 1990. It was added in 1880 to the house by Edith Arendup (a Courtauld) as a Mass centre for the few Catholics then in Wimbledon. Sadly, it has now been pulled down.

had become, 'one of the most familiar and best beloved figures in Wimbledon'. As the cortège passed through the town centre to the cemetery at Gap Road, large crowds lined the route and all shops were closed as a mark of respect. At the graveside there were not only his fellow priests, but the Anglican Vicar of Wimbledon, Canon Bell, and the minister of the Baptist Church in Queen's Road, the Revd Charles Ingrem.

This marked a welcome change in local attitudes towards religion. In 1837 there was only one church, the Anglican parish church, St Mary's. Otherwise there was 'a very small Dissenting chapel' off the High Street and an equally tiny Roman Catholic chapel in the grounds of The Keir on Westside. Successive Vicars, above all Canon Henry Haygarth, tried to maintain this Anglican predominance in face of the ever-growing population by building ten new churches (from Christ Church, Cottenham Park, in 1859 to St Peter's off Hartfield Road in 1911), as well as additional parish schools. They achieved a great deal, especially the 'kindly, open and sincere' Haygarth,

who lived for the parish that he served for over forty years (1859-1902). But many of the new residents were not attracted to their services; they found them 'dull'.

Consequently for the first time Nonconformists flourished in Wimbledon. Between 1883 (the opening of the large Congregational church in Worple Road) and 1914 they outbuilt the Anglicans. In just thirty years the Methodists, Baptists and Presbyterians, as well as the Congregationalists and Roman Catholics constructed thirteen new churches and chapels, above all in South Wimbledon. A religious census, carried out in 1903, showed that taken together there were nearly 8,000 at their services on the chosen Sunday, whereas the Anglicans drew under 6,000. The largest congregation was at the fine new Baptist church in Queens Road where Sunday after Sunday a thousand came to hear the Revd Charles Ingrem.

The religious census, however, revealed one other disconcerting statistic. Despite reports that their services were 'full to overflowing', only a third of the local population were counted as being in church on census Sunday. The same unpalatable fact had been revealed by the only other religious census in 1851, but then there had been just one church in Wimbledon, recognised as being too small. In 1903 there were 23. For the first time in history a sizeable number of the inhabitants (not merely in Wimbledon, but all over London) did not bother to go to church; some even rejected Christianity altogether. Such a conclusion was clearly of greater significance than all the other developments in the Edwardian borough.

Life in a Surburb between the Wars

EFFECT OF THE WAR

Whether they went to church or not, the vast majority of local people between the wars kept 11 am on 11 November, Armistice Day, as a very special moment at which to remember those who had died in the First World War. Compared to the war that started in 1939, that of 1914-18 inflicted little local damage. Only one bomb was dropped on the Borough and it did not go off. A large area of the Common had been taken over as an Army training camp, but within a few years most people had forgotten where the huts used to be. The Royal Wimbledon Golf Club had given up two of the holes on its course as a pasture for sheep and a plot for growing potatoes, but they were soon restored.

Yet no previous war had had such a profound local effect. Many families lost a father or a son; some like that of Canon Bell, the Vicar of St Mary's, lost two sons in quick succession early in 1918. The lives of those who returned home had often been dramatically changed by their experiences –

166. The dedication of the War Memorial, Parkside, on Sunday 5 November 1921. Designed by Sir Thomas Jackson, it was unveiled by Sir Joseph Hood, MP for Wimbledon. Canon Monroe, Vicar of St Mary's, leads a religious service with his parish choir.

167. Copse Hill, only a narrow bridleway below the hospitals when this postcard was published in 1908. Yet it must have had enough traffic to justify an early road sign. It was first widened in 1925 and provided with 'traffic calming measures' in 1998.

A TYPICAL SUBURB

Within a few years, however, the Borough had outwardly recovered and with some reason could claim to 'rank as one of the best residential suburban areas'. In fact, in his book *The Twenties* published in 1957, J. Montgomery placed his typical suburban family – a thirty-year-old stockbroker, his wife and their one son – in Wimbledon in 1925. The father chose the district because it was so close to London, yet thanks to the Common had managed to retain its 'semi-rural character'. Without a car, he depended on public transport and so used the fast, cheap train service to Waterloo (with a three monthly season ticket costing just under three pounds). His wife liked the shops in Hill Road and the Broadway, which, she felt 'catered for all tastes' and gave her no problem carrying the goods home as most were still delivered. Husband and wife also had no fears for their son's education as Wimbledon was noted for its variety of good private schools.

The official town guides published in the 1920s and '30s give interesting additional information on the type of suburb such a family was choosing. In 1921 it had been 'suffering from a dearth of houses as a result of the suspension of building operations during the War'. By 1925, however, 'modern, well-built' houses were going up once

168. Holland Gardens, Cottenham Park, in the 1930s. Once a field belonging to the Hollands who lived at Holmhurst to the north, it was given to the Council in 1929 as a Recreation Ground.

as a prisoner of war, as a victim of a gas attack, as an ex-serviceman with a permanent injury. They could look at the long lists of those killed in action inscribed on war memorials (and in the Warrior Chapel in St Mary's church) and see the names of relatives and friends. Their memories were passed on to those born between the Wars. So no Wimbledonian could escape the influence of the War, even if it was only 'the chronic servant problem' complained about by wealthier families.

169. The new All-England grounds, Church Road, from the air in 1929. Once part of the Spencers' Dairy Farm, it had been opened by George V in 1922. In the foreground is the Wimbledon Park golf course; to the right of the Centre Court is John Barker's sports field; to the left are Somerset and Burghley Roads with their large Victorian mansions.

more in the Devas estate off Pepys Road and the Drax estate off Copse Hill, and they could be bought (with garages) for just over £1000. There was also now no danger of the 'character of the population' changing as had been feared when trams first arrived, since 'the Borough is now built over so far as the cheaper class of houses is concerned' (which meant that families wanting such homes had to settle in new suburbs to the south, such as Morden and St Helier). Moreover, 'the policy of the local authority is to maintain the Borough as a residential district'. It is 'non-industrial' and has 'every prospect of remaining so'.

INDUSTRIES AND ESTATE AGENTS

Strictly speaking this claim was not true. For centuries along the river Wandle there had flourished three important Wimbledon mills – the oldest, a flour mill with a large pond near Merton High Street; a copper mill with a huge waterwheel by Plough Lane; and near Wandsworth a calico print works that in 1871 had employed nearly 200 men, women and girls. By the 1920s the print works had ceased operating, but the other two had become prosperous leather mills – Connolly Brothers who made leather upholstery for cars, and Chuter and Sons Chamois Leather Dressers. Near by during the later nineteenth century other works had been added – a Gas Works in North Road and the Municipal Power Station in Durnsford Road, along with a mineral water manufacturers in Caxton Road. In addition, by the 1920s there was a whole string of small industrial works along the north side of Kingston Road – manufacturing chemists, fountain pen makers, coach and motor body builders and the Southdown Laundry with its high chimney (brought down with great skill in the 1960s).

Admittedly, all these works were just inside Wimbledon's boundary with Merton, Mitcham and Tooting. But the Southdown Laundry was only the most southerly of a whole string of laundries across the Borough. In the days before washing machines and laundrettes, they were much in demand and provided a good service with weekly collections and deliveries by van. Among them, the best known were the Bendon Sanitary Laundry, Caxton Road, the Wimbledon Laundry, Cranbrook Road, and the Beulah Laundry, West Place. Next door to the Beulah was a competitor, the Cleveland, run almost single-handed by Mrs Muir. She worked long hours, doing the washing, putting it through a mangle, drying the towels and sheets on lines strung across the Common and then delivering the ironed washing in an old pram.

The town guides naturally chose to ignore such industry, even though the laundries were then an essential aid to middle-class life. Estate agents followed their example and instead stressed their work as 'The Wimbledon Homefinders'. There were a good number of them, especially in the High Street and near the Station. The earliest seems to have been set up by an ex-carpenter and builder, Daniel Mason, whose grandfather Samuel had managed The Rose and Crown in the late eighteenth century. In the 1840s he rebuilt several cottages in West Place and proclaimed himself 'Surveyor and Estate Agent'. He was followed in the 1870s by Michael Ogden who started as a butcher in the High Street, and then by Hawes and Co. 'established 1885', followed around 1910 by Cross and Prior, and Bateman. Rather aloof stood the London firm of Hampton's, who came in 1900 to develop the Wimbledon House Parkside estate and saw 'an enormous demand for high-class residences with tennis courts and motor houses'. By 1912 they had sold 98 of the 100 houses already built - mainly to doctors, lawyers and company directors.

NEW RESIDENTS

One doctor who brought his young family to Wimbledon was Cecil Cloake. He had had his medical studies interrupted by service in the Army on the Western Front and had gained a Military Cross at the Somme. In 1923 he settled in Queens Road as member of a medical practice of three doctors, serving both private patients who came in at the front door, and the poorer 'panel' patients who sat on hard wooden benches by a side entrance. He had no nurse or secretary or receptionist. He kept all medical records himself and his wife or the maid answered the door and the telephone. Every weekday, morning and evening, as well as Saturday mornings, he held a surgery. In the afternoons he did his 'house-calls', at first on a bicycle, but soon in a Morris tourer with a canvas hood. He had never driven a car before and there was then no driving test. So after a few tips from his brother-in-law, he drove off – and never had an accident.

His wife used Blunt's Market in Hartfield Road. The butcher, Albert Pearce, was resplendent in striped overall and boater. On the counter was his great chopping-block and an array of meat cleavers; the floor was covered in sawdust. Over the bridge, not yet lined with shops, was Elys which had 'one of those splendid overhead rail systems for speeding cash and bills to and from a central cashier's desk'. The assistant would place money and bill into a little cup, pull a plug and the cup would shoot along the rails, to return with the receipt and change. Over the road was Boots, not long in Hill Road and for many like the Cloakes as much used for its large subscription library of new books as for its chemist's department.

Their young son was more interested in Long's, a sweet- and toyshop near the top of Hartfield Road. The sweets were kept in large glass jars and had to be weighed and funnelled into little paper bags. Nothing then was pre-packaged except the chocolate bars. The toys were just as enticing – 'shelves packed with deep red boxes of Britain's soldiers and brighter red boxes of Hornby train sets'. He was also intrigued by the smells special to almost every shop, especially ground coffee in the grocer's and fresh butter and cream in the dairy. He loved travelling by tram up to London for half-price (a penny) and by bus to Putney on the open-topped 93s. When the trolleybuses appeared in 1931, he was amazed to see the conductor producing the ticket from a machine on a paper roll, instead of from a rack of coloured tickets and a tinkling punch as the bus conductors did.

When old enough to go to school, he was taken on foot by his mother for the first term or two. But then he was trusted to go on his own as the traffic was not very heavy, and later he rode there on his bicycle. At school, like many in his class, he collected stamps and cigarette cards. Stamps could be bought at Russell's, the photographers who had moved in 1936 to a shop just by the newly-opened Odeon Cinema in Worple Road. For cigarette cards he had to rely on his father smoking the right brand – 'and at least once he had to change to satisfy the demand for particular cards'.

The Cloake family also noticed other features of the streets in the 1930s which have now disappeared – rag-and-bone men pushing their barrows or driving their rickety carts, knife-grinders sitting on the pavement using a treadle-operated grindstone, French onion-sellers on their bicycles with strings of onions round their shoulders, barrel-organs sometimes with a monkey, Punch and Judy shows in St Mark's Place near the Library, and every summer Wall's ice cream 'stop me and buy one' salesmen on their tricycles.

Like the Cloakes, many other families settled in Wimbledon during the 1920s and '30s. Among them were those who bought houses in a new road laid out in 1922 on the remains of the Mount Ararat estate and named Devas after its last owner. Eighteen detached houses, selling at around £1000 each, with quite sizeable gardens were put up by a number of builders and in a variety of styles. The earliest were not provided with garages; the final ones built between 1925 and 1928 were. At first few were used and until well into the 1930s tradesmen's carts and bicycles were seen in the

road rather than cars. The area was obviously quiet and select, especially for the ladies 'of independent means' who bought one of the first houses. But most of the householders had settled there for a variety of other reasons: nearness to Raynes Park station for a businessman, a civil servant and an Air Commodore working at the Air Ministry; convenience to a local business for a laundry manager and a builder; and the fact that a Roman Catholic school was less than a mile away for the sons of a commercial traveller.

Unlike their Edwardian predecessors they experienced few 'days never to be forgotten'. In May 1926 the General Strike produced little trouble in Wimbledon as it was hardly an industrial area, though the National Union of Railwaymen held meetings in the Broadway and on the Common. The previous summer far more interest had been taken in a great historical pageant and fair held over three brilliantly sunny days in the grounds of Wimbledon Park House – 'by kind permission of HSH Princess Wiasemsky of Russia'. The Princess in fact was better known as the daughter of Gordon Selfridge and had married a White Russian prince and aviator. Supported by Selfridge money, they settled in the old Spencer manor house in 1923 and every summer held a large fête in the grounds for a local charity. But in 1936 the Selfridge fortune ran out and the Wiasemskys had to leave the house, which developed dry rot and finally had to be pulled down in 1949.

More significant for the future were the improvements in transport – the rebuilding of Wimbledon Station in 1929 which brought the main and District lines together under one roof; the opening in 1930 of a new line to Sutton via Wimbledon Chase; and the start the following year of a trolley-bus service to Hampton Court replacing the trams. Cars also benefited from the first petrol pumps at garages, installed in the early 1920s – though the very first at the Wimbledon Motor Works drew such crowds that the Council had to order its removal. But the increasing traffic in the town centre led in 1934 to the first traffic lights (installed on the still dangerous corner of Hill and Alexandra Roads) and to the Belisha beacon crossings (named after the Minister of Transport, Leslie Hore-Belisha, who later lived at Warren Farm).

Local controversies too were never far away. The opening in 1928 of the Wimbledon Stadium on Plough Lane for greyhound and speedway racing drew strong criticism from lovers of more traditional sports. The plan to allow cinemas to open on Sundays led to violent opposition, especially from some Nonconformists, and was rejected at a public poll in 1933 – only to be accepted

170. Wimbledon Stadium, Plough Lane, from the air in 1929. It had been opened a year earlier as the first stadium in the London area for the new sports of greyhound and motor-cycle racing. The Wimbledon football ground is at the top right, with the river Wandle and the buildings of the old Copper Mill just to its left. The river is crossed by a bridge. The buildings of the Mill are below this. In the foreground is Summerstown.

two years later. Even the building in 1936 of the first purpose-built flats – Edge Hill Court and Emerson and Hill Courts on Wimbledon Hill – met with cries of protest.

A NEW TOWN HALL

Rather more important, however, was the opening of a new Town Hall in November 1931. The old Local Board Offices had proved quite inadequate for the extra work of a Borough Council. So in 1923 a Committee was formed under Alderman Bathgate to draw up a scheme for a new civic centre. They invited architects 'of British nationality' to submit designs, with a prize of £200 for the best. One hundred and fourteen did so and the plans of A.J. Hope, a Lancastrian, won as they showed 'architectural quality of the highest order'. The building work started in 1929 and took just eighteen months to complete. The new Town Hall along with its fine Civic Hall provided a

dignified and practical centre for local government, as well as for public meetings and concerts.

The building of the two Halls coincided with the start of the serious economic slump of the early 1930s. Inevitably it was criticised for wasting public money at a time of crisis. In fact the money (£200,000) was borrowed and the building provided work for men who would otherwise have been unemployed. As it was, Wimbledon, not being an industrial area, was spared the worst of the suffering. By 1931 there were about 2,000 people unemployed in the Borough, out of a total population of nearly 60,000. They were mainly clerks, shop assistants and labourers, and they staged several marches up the Broadway. Most people however, especially north of the railway, hardly noticed that there was a slump and in the General Elections of 1931 and 1935 gave the sitting National Government MP, Sir John Power, first 80, then 65 per cent of the votes against the Labour candidate, Tom Braddock.

171. *The second Town Hall from the air not long after its opening in 1931. To the left is the new railway station, though there are still no shops on the bridge. Behind the Town Hall is the Civic Hall, Baptist church and fire station, with the police station opposite on the corner of South Park Road.*

172. *The opening of the new Wimbledon Swimming Baths, Latimer Road, on 21 June 1929.*

173. *The eastern end of Worple Road photographed from the Alexandra on 2 October 1933. On the left is Elys which had celebrated its Golden Jubilee seven years earlier with a banquet in the store. Beyond are the small shops now covered by Sainsburys. On the right are the reconstructed shops on the Pavement, with Elys Furniture Store, soon to be rebuilt with a new Odeon Cinema alongside. Trolleybus wires hang over the road.*

174. *Members of the ARP near the War Memorial on the Common in the summer of 1939 demonstrating the dangers of a gas attack. Gas was then feared even more than bombs. So everyone was issued with a gas mask and the tops of pillar boxes were coated with a special green paint, meant to show the presence of gas.*

The Blackout, the Blitz and the Home Guard

THE BLACKOUT

If the twenty years between the Wars contained few events 'never to be forgotten', the six during the Second World War more than made up for this. From 3 September 1939 and Chamberlain's almost self-pitying announcement that war had been declared, to 8 May 1945 and Churchill's triumphant declaration that victory in Europe was complete, hardly a month passed without some memorable or tragic event. Listening to the radio for news, above all at 9pm, became almost a ritual for families who earlier had taken little interest in world affairs. Yet day-to-day life during the war was far more humdrum, a matter of enduring the unending difficulties posed by a long emergency.

One of the first problems from start to very nearly the finish was the blackout. On 1 September 1939 the government decreed that no lights must shine out from any building or vehicle, to deprive German bombers of an easy way of locating their targets. All windows had to be covered with thick curtains or boarded up; all street lighting was banned; cars could use only side-lights, while traffic lights were covered except for a tiny cross; trains ran with blinds down and compartments lit with a small blue light; buses had their windows covered with thick gauze and only a tiny slit left open to show passengers where they were. Air raid wardens were given the task of enforcing the orders and, like Warden Hodges in *Dad's Army*, became very unpopular, knocking even on friends' doors and demanding 'Put that light out!'. If their request was ignored, courts could inflict heavy fines.

Such draconian laws had quickly to be modified. In the first month of the war, road casualties doubled, so civilians were allowed to go out with a torch, whose beam had been dimmed by a layer of tissue paper. Cars could use headlights, masked by a hood with small slits to let out a minimum of light. Cyclists also were allowed to use a hooded lamp. Kerbs at corners and crossing places were painted white, as were the centres of roads, while street lamps were given bands of white to help those out at night. Nonetheless, most people still tried to get home before dark.

Churches with large, numerous windows were in a very awkward position. It was often too difficult or too expensive to black them out properly. So at the Sacred Heart, Edge Hill for instance, the solution was a 'dim-out'. On the altar there was a small hooded reading-lamp for the priest to see the missal and in the nave long flexes hung down from the main lights and to these were fixed small black lanterns with a blue bulb. They gave only a vague, eerie light, barely enough for the congregation to see the outline of the benches, let alone read a prayer book. In many churches in fact the only solution was to avoid the hours of darkness for services.

On top of the blackout, rationing was another unpleasant feature. In 'the Kaiser's War' it had only started in March 1918 and then just for meat, butter and margarine. In 'Hitler's War' it began in January 1940 for bacon, butter and sugar, and soon included most articles of food, above all meat, eggs and cheese, as well as clothes and sweets. To make matters worse, shopkeepers no longer delivered goods. They were assured of customers as families now had to register with them if they wanted, for example, meat and eggs, and could not go elsewhere. There were queues to be endured but the long lines of women were not made happier by seeing favoured customers (known locally as 'dearies') getting 'under-the-counter' extras like sausages. One way of having food 'off the ration' was to go to one of the new British Restaurants. The first in Wimbledon was opened in Holy Trinity church hall on the Broadway in October 1940 and others followed in Merton Road, Haydons Road, Arthur Road, Coombe Lane and the High Street. Reasonable meals could be had there for as little as a shilling. In addition, many people joined the 'Dig for Victory' campaign and grew their own vegetables in one of the new allotments started in public parks and on the Common. Others formed Pig Clubs, helped by kitchen scraps left in 'piggy-bins' at street corners.

A further worry were the blue identity cards with a personal number which were issued to everyone (partly to help with the distribution of ration books). Like gas masks, they were meant to be carried at all times and had to be produced if asked for by the police or by troops at a checkpoint. In the autumn of 1940, at a time when the authorities were on the look-out for possible spies, Home Guards at a post by the Lower Downs railway tunnel arrested an elderly man with a

175. A British Restaurant in Wimbledon. It was decorated with a mural by John Piper which has since disappeared.

strong foreign accent who could not produce his identity card. He was taken under escort to Wimbledon Police Station under suspicion of being an enemy spy. But there he was finally able to convince the Inspector that he was a Maltese Roman Catholic priest out on a sick call.

Thus every member of the family was closely affected by the war, but perhaps the worst off were the children. The education of many in both public and private schools was disrupted by evacuation and though the transport of children and teachers early in September 1939 to 'reception centres' in Kent, Sussex and Hampshire was well-organised, few really settled in their new homes and most returned to Wimbledon in the spring of 1940. Then came the Blitz which meant both frequent visits to the shelters where it was difficult to work, and nights when it was difficult to sleep. Games too were hindered by the need to clear sports fields of jagged pieces of shrapnel before matches could even begin and all after-school activities like clubs and plays had to be abandoned. The numbers of pupils in most schools were also lower than usual, younger teachers were called up and new books were almost impossible to obtain.

So quite apart from the depressing news of the war, life in Wimbledon was often grim. Eileen Bowen, who lived in Palmerston Road during the war, remembers that 'everyone got tired and shabby and hungry'. Yet, she maintains, 'they were friendlier and helped each other more'. All were 'suffering the same deprivations, the same shortages, and felt they were all in it together'. Trains and trams were often late and crowded, journeys took ages, but 'most people were patient'. They were cheered up by regular visits to the cinema and by humorous topical shows on the wireless, above all Tommy Handley's ITMA. So Eileen Bowen concludes: 'Life was hard, but it was also exciting'.

THE BLITZ

It was certainly exciting and at times very frightening during the summer of 1940. Until the middle of August people in Wimbledon had only known of the war at second-hand through the radio or the experiences of survivors from Dunkirk. Then just after tea on Thursday 16 August without any warning the anti-aircraft guns in Prince George's playing-fields in Raynes Park opened up on planes hidden in thick cloud. Probably in reply the first bombs dropped, small fifty-pounders, most likely meant for Croydon Airport. They fell along Merton High Street, Kingston Road and adjoining streets, damaging houses, destroying gas and water mains, setting fire to a tyre dump – and killing fourteen people. Among them was Terence Rosewell, a fourteen-year-old Wimbledon College boy. He was trying to get back to his home in Graham Road when bombs fell in front of and behind him. He was severely injured and died from his wounds in hospital. More fortunate was the elderly man said to have been found wandering among the ruins of his house. He held a lavatory chain and complained: 'All I did was to pull it and the whole bloody house fell down'.

For the rest of August and early September the air battle continued. Sometimes the planes could be seen, specks just visible in the blue sky, with the noise of their dives punctuated by the rat-a-tat of machine guns. But no more bombs fell in the borough. Then on the night of 7/8 September the London docks were set ablaze. The fire could be seen clearly from Wimbledon, a bright red glow across the eastern horizon, and over the next few days gardens were covered with blackened pieces of paper. The following night the bombers returned, this time to Wimbledon. They hit the station; the marks of bomb splinters can still be seen in the wall beside the District Line.

The Blitz had started. For the next three months without a night's break the raids went on and on. The sirens would go about 6.30pm, while searchlights probed the sky. The AA guns would start firing and then the regular hum of the German planes could be heard far overhead, apparently quite untroubled by the reaction below. Every so often there would be the screech of a bomb dropping, a violent explosion and the start of a new fire. For a time there was a brief lull. Then the noise started again, only to fade away before dawn. The all-clear finally sounded about 7.30am.

During the Blitz about 400 high-explosive, oil and petrol bombs, as well as thousands of incendiaries, fell on Wimbledon. Most seem to have been dropped at random as the German airmen flew towards central London. Yet there were important targets in the borough, especially the

176. A shop on the corner of the Broadway and Stanley Road, wrecked by a bomb on 15 September 1940. Later another bomb fell on the same unfortunate building.

station, the main railway line and the power-station at Durnsford Road. All were hit, but never put out of action. Far worse was the damage to and destruction of ordinary homes, especially along Haydons Road and along Gladstone and Russell Roads in South Wimbledon. Surprisingly few people were killed, thanks to the shelters and to the efficiency of the rescue services, directed from a command centre under the Town Hall. But the people who had to spend night after night in crowded shelters have never forgotten the experience. Eileen Bowen with her family was able to take refuge in the Town Hall. At first they had to sit on benches in a corridor, but then they were given tickets for a place on a bunk. 'My bunk', she later remembered, 'was right near a ventilator and I could hear every plane, bomb and all the gunfire. We would come out in the morning and find the Broadway thick with smoke, sometimes with debris and firemen's hoses everywhere'.

Wimbledon's heaviest raid was on the night of 6 November 1940. 67 high-explosive bombs fell in the hour after 7.30pm. They hit roads and houses all over the borough, but the most serious incident was at Queens Road School, used as the centre of the rescue and ambulance services. Four ambulances and a mobile first-aid unit were destroyed, while others could not get out because of rubble. As a result, the Civil Defence services were 'stretched to their absolute limit', yet remarkably only four people were killed and seven seriously injured. The final raid came six months later on 10 May 1941 when central London was nearly destroyed by fire. Wimbledon escaped

177. The Revd Robert Eke and some of the congregation of St Matthew's church, Durham Road, in front of the ruins on the fourth anniversary of its destruction by a flying bomb in June 1944. The church has since been rebuilt.

relatively lightly, but there were no trains to London the next day and gas and electricity were cut off for a time.

Over the nine months that the Blitz had lasted, nearly six hundred houses in the borough had been destroyed and over 2000 badly damaged. About 150 people had been killed and 440 seriously injured. On the other hand the German airmen had been able to cruise above the streets of Wimbledon with almost complete impunity. Despite the deafening AA barrage (especially from the 4.5 inch naval gun near the Windmill) which was meant to hearten civilians as well as force the planes to fly higher, only one bomber, a Junkers 88, seems to have been hit by gunfire. It crashed near the Nelson Hospital in September 1940. Otherwise the barrage certainly terrified as many civilians as did the bombs. Moreover it showered the area with jagged steel splinters and large nose-cones which damaged roofs all over the borough. Two planes did crash in Wimbledon – a Junkers 88 on a garden in Denmark Road on 16 April 1941

and three weeks later a Heinkel III on the first fairway of the Royal Wimbledon golf course (just behind Cannizaro Park). Both were shot down by Beaufighters.

THE HOME GUARD

By May 1941 Hitler was far more concerned with invading the Soviet Union. The British Army, however, was still worried by the danger of German invasion here, and so the Commander of Home Forces, General Sir Alan Brooke, was ready to assign an increasingly important part to the Home Guard. The Local Defence Volunteers had first been formed in May 1940 after a radio appeal by Sir Anthony Eden, then Secretary of State for War. In Wimbledon a distinguished First World War veteran, Lieut.-Col. W. Tenison DSO, was asked to form a local battalion and within four days he was able to hold the first parade with 200 volunteers. A year later he had 1,500 men under his command, complete with their own weapons.

178. An imaginative Home Guard exercise near the Common in 1943. The soldiers behind the fence on the left are defending the house against a German paratroop attack, represented by the dummy tank and fellow Home Guards dressed in Nazi uniform.

They held frequent combined exercises with battalions from Mitcham and neighbouring areas of London and they especially practised defending the Common against the long-expected arrival of enemy parachutists. The Common had already been criss-crossed with posts and trenches to try and prevent the landing of German gliders, while neighbouring roads had been partly blocked by concrete 'dragon's teeth' as a barrier to their tanks and a brick 'pill-box' had been concealed in the old Pound by Parkside to catch unwary storm-troopers. On top of these precautions General Brooke wanted the Home Guard to do more than just harass the Germans. He ordered the creation of 'nodal points' or defended localities where they would fight till overwhelmed, so as to give the Home Army time to mount a counter-attack. The local defended locality was apparently to be West Place on the edge of the Common.

The Home Guard was not composed simply of 'grizzled veterans'. Among its most enthusiastic members were those in the special platoon from King's College School Officers' Training Corps. They felt they were 'better armed and trained' than

179. The final Home Guard parade in November 1944. After a service in the Regal Cinema (now the Odeon) on the Broadway, they had marched over the railway bridge to salute the London area commanding officer, Major-General Sir D. Collins by a bomb-scarred Elys.

180. A small prisoner-of-war camp on Southside, photographed in 1946 with Chester House in the background. Italians and later Germans were kept in the few huts opposite the end of Lauriston Road. In their spare time they built this wooden model of the Windmill.

most in the Home Guard. Above all they had bicycles and so were given a mobile role, trying to prevent the German paratroops reaching the containers with their heavy weapons. Every Sunday morning they trained hard until they knew every track on the Common, then adjourned to The Crooked Billet or The Hand-in-Hand for a glass of beer and a smoke. From 1943 the battalion also recruited ladies known as 'Women Auxiliaries', but what exactly their job was has yet to be revealed. Only a year later with the threat of invasion long vanished, the work of the Home Guard was over and in November 1944 the force 'stood down' after a final parade along the Broadway and Hill Road.

That summer their last task had been to carry out 'anti-loot patrols' after many more houses had been damaged. The final twist in the War happened just as the D-Day landings in northern France seemed on the verge of success. The Germans unleashed one of the most unnerving of all their secret weapons, the pilot-less bomb-carrying plane or V-1. Almost every morning from 16 June to 28 August 1944 a number of these 'Doodlebugs', with

their unmistakable noise and fire in their tails, passed overhead in the direction of London. Most went over, but about 40 came down in Wimbledon (compared to about 142 that fell in Croydon). Each damaged on average three to five hundred houses, as it exploded on contact and so the blast was felt over a wide area. 'If it came near,' Eileen Bowen recalled, 'you stopped, listened for it to cut out, ducked and prayed that it wasn't your turn'.

The first fell on Cliveden Road, completely destroying seventeen houses and killing twelve people. The last passed over Wimbledon; then its engine stopped and it made a complete turn, heading back towards Cottenham Park. It plunged to earth on Lambton Road and Amity Grove, where it flattened more houses, but fortunately only killed two people. Overall, the total casualties were lighter than expected – 36 killed and 252 injured, but nearly half the houses in the borough had been damaged. As in every 'battle' there were lighter moments. During morning Mass at the Sacred Heart church with its huge windows, an elderly priest, hearing the noise of yet another V-1 overhead, could contain himself no longer. He started to thump the altar, shouting: 'Damn those Germans! Damn those Germans!'.

The Lord must have listened as only nine months later the war in Europe finally came to an end. Churchill's announcement of VE Day on 8 May 1945 set off joyful celebrations all over the country. In South Wimbledon street parties were quickly organised for the children. Eileen Bowen recalls that 'every household provided food of some sort. There was bunting everywhere'. The pubs were thronged, people danced in the streets and sellers of rosettes and VE ribbons at Wimbledon Station did a roaring trade. On the green at The Crooked Billet there was a giant bonfire with an effigy of Hitler on top. On the Common there were fireworks and the night sky was lit up by searchlights. Only at the Town Hall was there little sign of jollification as the Council had allocated just £100 to be spent on flags and bunting. The following Sunday there was a non-denominational Civic Service of thanksgiving in the Theatre and later the Civil Defence and Armed Services held a victory parade to the Town Hall.

The victory was seemingly total. Yet only three days after VE Day the editor of *The Boro' News* posed the vital question: 'What are we going to do with this peace?' Over fifty years later we know the answer locally, as well as nationally and internationally. It is certainly not what was widely expected in May 1945.

Four Members of Parliament

183. Arthur Palmer, Labour MP for Wimbledon 1945-50. His victory after the War caused a sensation. He was an engineer and spoke with authority on the electrical supply industry.

181. Rt Hon. Henry Chaplin, Conservative MP for Wimbledon 1907-16. Known as 'the squire', he was a typical country gentleman and had no previous connection with the Borough. In the 1880s he had been in the Cabinet, but in 1906 lost his seat in Lincolnshire. So Central Office found him a new one, Wimbledon, which he won easily against the Women's Suffrage candidate, Bertrand Russell. He won two more elections in 1910, but retired to the Lords in 1916.

182. Sir John Power, Conservative MP 1924-45, second from the right in this picture taken in the Mayor's parlour at the opening of a War Savings Week in 1944. Power did not live in Wimbledon and is said never to have made a speech in the Commons. The dominant personality here is Lady Roney, next to Power and Wimbledon's only lady Mayor (1933-35).

184. Sir Cyril Black, Conservative MP 1950-70. He was a local councillor, Mayor (1945-47) and a member of the Surrey County Council. He was a staunch campaigner against the permissive society and the creation of the London Borough of Merton. He won six elections but with decreasing majorities.

Where is Merton?

RECOVERY FROM THE WAR

Wimbledon survived the War and also 'the years of austerity' after 1945. It has even survived over a quarter of a century as part of a London Borough it never wanted to join. Now in April 1998 *The Wimbledon News* has reported a meeting between the local Member of Parliament, Roger Casale, and businessmen who want the Borough named Wimbledon instead of Merton – so as to promote trade. 'Wimbledon has a high-profile name', one of them claimed, 'Merton is very historical, but not many people would be able to tell you where it is' – a remark echoing the question said once to have been asked by a very senior member of the Royal Family on a visit to the area. She had clearly heard of Wimbledon, but asked: 'Where is Merton?'

The link with Merton, Morden and Mitcham since 1965 in the London Borough of Merton has come to dominate Wimbledon's recent history. Yet for the first twenty years after the end of the War the town managed quite reasonably on its own. Like every other place in England in the late 1940s, it suffered continued food and clothes rationing, a ban on the building of private houses (hardly replaced by the 71 'prefabs' put up on bombed sites) and a shortage of fuel, above all during the 'big freeze' in early 1947 when there was hard frost on 27 successive nights, cinemas only opened at 4pm and street lights were turned off at midnight.

In the 1950s the housing situation improved. A new council estate was developed behind Chester and Westside Houses on the Common, while along Parkside many of the Victorian mansions (like Lincoln House) were pulled down and their grounds filled with small 'town houses'. South Wimbledon too became more attractive after the disappearance of the old gas, sewage and electricity works, and the ending of smogs through the introduction of a smokeless zone. Many of the terraced Victorian houses were renovated; some were replaced by small blocks of flats. Along the Broadway, traffic was able to flow more freely thanks to the disappearance of trams early in January 1951. All over the Borough the growing national prosperity was shown in the increasing number of private cars, the opening of a Sainsbury's store in Worple Road, the sprouting of television aerials on many more chimneys, especially after the Queen's Coronation in 1953 – and the consequent closure of the majority of local cinemas, except the Regal (renamed the Odeon) in the Broadway.

In 1955, however, came the first sign of impend-

185. The scene outside the Town Hall in May 1988 when the Wimbledon football team came onto the balcony to show the FA Cup to their enthusiastic supporters.

186.   *The bottom of Hill Road in the 1970s before it was redeveloped. The original large houses are still there, except for the one that Mr Ely bought, but the coal merchants' offices have disappeared from the station forecourt.*

ing trouble. The Council celebrated the fiftieth anniversary of the granting of Wimbledon's Charter. The Mayor declared that 'The Borough has progressed', proved by the great increase in the value of local property. Unfortunately, few of the citizens seemed very interested in the official celebrations, which happened to coincide with a rail strike and a week of poor weather, and so were poorly attended. Some people even wondered what all the fuss was about.

BOROUGH NUMBER 22
Eight years later there was far greater fuss in Wimbledon over a plan to reorganise the government of London in the interests, it was claimed, of greater economy and efficiency. Wimbledon was to be transferred from the county of Surrey to the new county of Greater London, as part of Borough 'Number 22', along with Merton, Morden and Mitcham. The idea of a merger with Merton and Morden was not new. It had been suggested in 1919 by Wimbledon Council and made sense, as over the centuries there had been many links with Merton, notably Nelson's 'Paradise' which had been as much in Wimbledon as in Merton. But it was turned down by the other authorities, who feared domination by their wealthier neighbour. The merger with Mitcham, however, was a very

different matter. The river Wandle had proved a more effective barrier over the centuries than the Kingston Road and, apart from a few landowners like Henry Hoare in the 1770s who owned property in both parishes, relations had not been particularly close. Its addition to Borough 22 seemed therefore a matter of administrative convenience, simply to make up numbers.

There was inevitably a bitter dispute over the name of the new Borough. As the town with what their council claimed was 'the largest service area' and with 'a national and even international reputation', Wimbledon expected that its name would be chosen. But this idea was strongly opposed by Merton and Mitcham on the grounds of their declared 'enmity' to Wimbledon and fear of a takeover of the new authority by the very influential brothers, Sir Cyril and Sydney Black. The Minister of Housing and Local Government therefore proposed the name Merton because of its 'historical associations' with the medieval priory and with Lord Nelson. Wimbledon Council then took their case to the Privy Council, but lost. So 'in the interests of harmony' they suggested a joint name, Wimbledon and Merton, on the lines of Kensington and Chelsea. But the Minister refused to change his decision and the Chairman of Merton Council was delighted as 'it comes in the year of the seventh centenary celebrations of Merton

College, Oxford'.

So at the end of March 1965 Wimbledon Borough Council under its 34th Mayor, Councillor Ayres, held its final meeting and on 1 April the London Borough of Merton was born. The London Government Act was far from popular in the town. For four centuries Wimbledonians had been responsible for local affairs and many naturally feared that a larger, more remote authority would lead to greater bureaucracy and higher rates. These fears were voiced by their MP, Sir Cyril Black, the only Conservative member to vote against the Act in the Commons. When it finally came into operation, he declared that he went into 'the new venture hoping for the best, but fearing the worst', before adding defiantly: 'Wimbledon will live on; there is no question of it losing its unique character'.

187. The western end of Hill Road along with the shops on the bridge have been transformed by the St George's development of the 1980s, and the controversial 'Fridge on the Bridge' of the early 1990s. Since this picture was taken in 1995, even the cab rank has changed.

WIMBLEDON'S ENDURING CHARACTER

That special character has certainly survived and in some ways been strengthened. It had evolved over centuries and could not be destroyed by government decree. In reaction to a local authority, criticised for being 'over-large, bureaucratic and remote from the people it is supposed to serve', residents' associations have sprung up in areas like Wimbledon Park, Copse Hill and the Village, and they are now linked by WURA (Wimbledon Union of Residents' Associations) to strengthen their representations to the Council. In addition, in 1982 the John Evelyn Society was renamed the Wimbledon Society to emphasise its declared aim 'to preserve and improve' local amenities, while its Planning Committee, including architects and town planning experts, has done its best to try and persuade the Council to ensure 'sympathetic and orderly' development.

Moreover, despite being officially labelled Merton, Wimbledon has retained a genuine sense of community. Perhaps, as one estate agent commented: 'It is a cosmopolitan community these days'. Nonetheless it has been shown at its best in the Wimbledon and Merton Council of Churches which has promoted much closer relations between local congregations, in the care for the elderly and those in need by the Guild of Social Welfare, and in the Community Centre in St George's Road, a meeting-place for innumerable groups and societies. It is equally evident in the great interest taken in the history of Wimbledon, especially since the opening of the Windmill Museum in 1976, the Lawn Tennis Museum the following year and the refurbished Wimbledon Society Museum in 1994.

The arts too have not been neglected since the War. The Wimbledon Symphony Orchestra, founded in 1949 by a local bank manager, Ken Tucker, and revived in the 1960s by Ken Jones, still flourishes under its conductor, John Alldis. The Choral Society, founded in 1914, has continued to give concerts, as have the Hill Singers. The Wimbledon Theatre has managed to survive despite several crises, while the Polka Children's Theatre in the Broadway was started in 1979, just before the sad ending of Eric Ward's Repertory Theatre which was known for its high standard in both acting and production.

In sport Wimbledon also became famous – and not only for the Tennis Championships. In 1988 the Football Club won the FA Cup at Wembley, 25 years after winning the Amateur Cup there and only two years after gaining promotion to the First Division of the Football League. The victorious team were given a rapturous reception when they returned to Wimbledon, above all at the Town Hall which fortunately was then still the civic centre. The Cricket Club, well over a hundred years old, has won the Surrey Club Championship on several occasions, while the revived Rugby XV, one of the original founders of the Rugby Union in the 1860s, reached the final of the Surrey Cup in 1997 and 1998, as well as regularly hosting half-marathons from its grounds off Copse Hill.

The magic name Wimbledon still excites estate agents and writers in the property pages of national newspapers. One described the High Street with its wide variety of eating places as 'reminiscent of the type of village found in Mills and Boon novels', while another felt 'Wimbledon tennis fame is a distraction from its real merits'. For him these were 'its Common, its four golf courses, its many excellent schools, its proximity to Central London

188. *The entrance to the new Centre Court shopping complex in 1995. The edge of the redundant Town Hall is on the right. The shops on the opposite side of the Broadway still occupy the original buildings of the 1870s, though all have a new use.*

and its quality housing'. Certainly property in Wimbledon commands exceptionally high prices, especially if it is advertised as 'London luxury combined with country living'. Over the years it has attracted people as diverse as Sir Jack Hobbs, the great Surrey cricketer (who lived in Dunstall Road), Air Chief Marshal Lord Dowding, the Battle of Britain commander (St Mary's Road), and Ethel Mannin, a leading novelist (Burghley Road), all of whom deserve to be commemorated by blue plaques on their houses.

CONTROVERSY OVER TOWN CENTRE

Yet, according to the Wimbledon Society, 'the history of the town's rejuvenation has regrettably been one of bungling, indecision and lost opportunities'. Even stronger criticism has come from the Victorian Society: 'Instead of a town of great character and obvious civic pride,' a new Town Centre has been built 'which could be found anywhere in the country'. On the other hand, the leading developers, Speyhawk Retail, strongly supported by Merton Council, proclaimed 'Centre Court', the heart of the Town Centre, 'the new shopping experience for the community', which with its large car park 'makes shopping a dream'.

Behind these conflicting views lay a totally different idea of Wimbledon's future. To Merton Council and above all to their planning department, the town no longer needed 'a civic presence'; they saw it primarily as 'the Borough's main retail and business centre'. Hence in 1983 they decided to remove the headquarters of the Council and all its staff to Crown House, Morden, a fourteen storey office-block in a more central

position in the Borough and large enough for all departments to be in one building for the first time. They also drew up a series of grandiose plans for the Town Centre, sweeping away old shops in St George's Road, along one side of the bridge, at the top of Hartfield Road and around the theatre, as well as the Town and Civic Halls, the Baptist church, Fire Station and Magistrates' Court. In their place was to be a major shopping, office and car parking scheme in St George's Road, four large new shops on the bridge, a monster seven storey office-block over the railway, a new theatre complex and above all a huge shopping centre on the Town Hall site. To deal with the extra traffic brought by the new shops and offices, there were also to be important changes to the road-system, including the building of an extra bridge over the railway to the east of the station, associated with another large office-block.

To many people in Wimbledon, on the other hand, this dramatic refashioning of their town, on the lines of Croydon or Kingston, seemed more like a nightmare. Their opposition was voiced by the Wimbledon Society, above all by its Chairman, Norman Plastow, an architect. He claimed that the real problem was that the Borough was now too large, with the result that only a minority of councillors had personal knowledge of local issues and so decisions on vital matters like the Town Centre were taken which were not supported by people in Wimbledon. In this way 'the civic presence and conveniently placed local services' had been eliminated from the town, whereas Wimbledon people wanted both to be 'locally available, locally accountable and locally visible'. To make matters worse the Council allowed 'bland and poorly conceived developments to replace good Victorian buildings in a conservation area'.

The bitter disputes over virtually every development led to a series of lengthy and expensive public enquiries. The most important, over the future of the Town Hall, did force the Council and Speyhawk to modify their plans and agree to retain virtually the entire building, as well as the facades of the Baptist church, Fire Station and Magistrate's Court. Other developments, especially the new bridge over the railway were abandoned because of their expense. But the Civic Hall was pulled down, despite a promise in the Town Centre plan that this would only happen when a contract had been signed for its replacement, while invaluable shops, like Hughes the ironmonger's, were compulsorily purchased to make way for 'a featureless, glass-clad, flat-roofed office block', the so-called 'Fridge on the Bridge'.

Of course, the Council had no monopoly on controversial developments. The 'New Look Elys'

189. The Civic Hall designed by A.J. Hope in 1931 to seat 1,400 people. It was pulled down in 1990 to make way for Centre Court and has yet to be replaced.

created in 1986 has claims to be the ugliest shop-front in the town, whereas Speyhawk's skilful adaptation of the Town Hall as a shopping centre with an imposing entrance rotunda has provided a focal point for the start of the Broadway. Moreover, in the last few years, leading councillors have begun to listen more to local views, especially on the urgent need for a new public hall to replace the one lost in 1990. Originally they had only wanted a small multi-purpose hall. In February 1998, however, they gave outline planning consent for a new Civic Hall to seat 800 people and be used as a conference, performance and community centre with a café, bar and basement car park. It will be built on the Hartfield Road car park site and run by a Trust in co-operation with the Council – so long as the scheme can attract outside financial support. Such a hall would give Wimbledon a real town centre, 'much more than somewhere to shop', and 'a genuine meeting-place' with provision for leisure and cultural activities.

'Every age', it is said, 'is an age of change'. Wimbledon residents in the past doubtless discussed and resented the changes they saw taking place round them. But in the past thirty years change has been taking place on a far greater scale and has come at a pace unknown before. Many people have been bewildered by the transforma-

tion of their town centre, the disappearance of small family shops, the threat to their hospitals and recreation grounds, the unending procession of cars and huge lorries, and the attempt to control them by so-called 'traffic calming' measures, above all a dangerous new 'slalom' on Copse Hill, as well as a controversial cycle track along Coombe Lane.

Yet amid all the changes, it is worth remembering that Victorian Wimbledon itself grew up haphazardly. Its town centre certainly developed by accident and could hardly be called attractive. Moreover, unlike Kingston and Croydon, a good number of buildings survive from the Georgian and Victorian periods, and are now partly protected in Conservation Areas which are spread all over the town. Even the small shops, which have seemed so much in danger especially in the Village, have managed to survive in districts like Cottenham Park (where Hartshorn's in Coombe Lane has been a butcher's since it opened in 1896, while Maher's in Durham Road still has the original bread oven of 1883). So Winifred Whitehead, in her evocative memories *Wimbledon 1885-1965*, was able to conclude that, though miserable at the destruction of her old home, Lauriston House, in 1959, and feeling that 'the whole neighbourhood has lost much of its dignity and serenity', Wimbledon remained ' a wonderfully pleasant place' in which to live.

Conclusion: The Museum of Wimbledon Past

The Wimbledon Society Museum of Local History is in itself sure evidence of the town's unique character. Opened just over eighty years ago in October 1916 during the First World War, it has always been a private museum and never had to rely on Council funds. It has also never had a home of its own. It started in the Reading Room of the Village Club at the corner of the Ridgway and Lingfield Road, and later moved to a larger room upstairs. It has been promised more suitable premises by the Council – notably in 1950 at Eagle House in the High Street and in the early 1980s at Cannizaro House on the Common. Sadly, both schemes fell through.

The fact that the Museum has not merely survived, but prospered is a tribute to the dedication of those who have served over the years on its Committee. Among the most notable are Richardson Evans, the founder of the Society in 1903 and once described as 'a man with a vision of Wimbledon', Margaret Grant, its first Curator, Bill Myson, Borough Librarian and Secretary of the Society, and Guy Parsloe, the President who organised the planning of a more modern display in 1973.

Twenty years later this display was itself transformed by Norman Plastow, the Society's Chairman, and Paul Bowness, an expert in museum design. Together they produced what became known as a 'refurbished mu-

190. The Village Club and Lecture Hall on the corner of the Ridgway and Lingfield Road in 1925. Designed by Samuel Teulon, they were opened in 1859 to provide 'opportunities of intellectual and moral improvement' through a reading room, library and lectures in the Hall (on the left). The Club still flourishes, though for very different reasons.

192. A memory of 'Wimbledon Past' in the Museum: a postcard of Beverley Way, part of the Kingston By-Pass, in the late 1930s, where today a flyover carries Coombe Lane above the unceasing traffic on the A3.

191. Richardson Evans (1846-1928). A leader-writer on The Pall Mall Gazette, he lived at The Keir on Westside and won strong support for the founding of the JohnEvelyn Club, one of the first local conservation societies. He led campaigns to preserve part of the old Village Green, Wandle Park as a public recreation ground and above all Beverley Meads or the 'Commons Extension'. For this work he was made the first Freeman of the Borough of Wimbledon in 1910.

seum'. For the first time visitors could see a complete history of Wimbledon through models, pictures, maps, display cases and large panels which explained the chief developments. In addition, those wanting to find more about the past could look in at an extra room added to the Museum and named the Perry Room after two generous donors. Here are kept the Society's library, maps, press-cuttings, ephemera, photographs and paintings, a massive collection of material invaluable for local historians, its full extent now only being realised thanks to the computer index made by Alan Elliot.

The refurbished Museum was opened on 8 July 1994 by the present Earl Spencer, then still lord of the manor. It has led to a great increase in the number of visitors, even though it is normally open only on Saturday afternoons and has no car park. It does, however, manage to extend its work to a much wider audience through an ever-increasing number of publications on local history and through its growing links with local schools. It is now planning to mark the Millennium with a new Photographic Survey of the entire town.

The official aim of the Museum is 'to collect, conserve, record and display material relating to the history of Wimbledon and make it available to all'. Wimbledon's Past is clearly now better cared for than ever before.

Further Reading

General Histories of Wimbledon

Bartlett, W: *The History and Antiquities of Wimbledon* (1865; 2nd edn 1971).

Cooke, A.A: *Old Wimbledon* (1927).

Milward, R.J: *A new Short History of Wimbledon* (1989).

Milward, R.J: *Historic Wimbledon: From Caesar's Camp to Centre Court* (1989).

Milward, R.J: *Wimbledon: A Pictorial History* (1994).

Plastow, N. (editor): *History of Wimbledon and Putney Commons* (1986).

Early Wimbledon

Bird, J. and D. (editors): *The Archaeology of Surrey to 1540* (1987).

Blair, J: *Early Medieval Surrey* (1991).

Milward, R.J: *Early and Medieval Wimbledon* (1984).

Milward, R.J: *The Rectory: Wimbledon's Oldest House* (1992).

Milward, R.J: *A Church since Domesday: St Mary's Wimbledon* (1993).

Tudor, Stuart and Georgian Wimbledon

Arnold, C: *Wimbledon's National Schools, 1733-1912* (1912).

Bridgwater, P: *Arnold Schopenhauer's English Schooling* (1988).

Cowe, F.M. (editor): *Wimbledon Vestry Minutes, 1743-1788* (1964).

Higham, C.S: *Wimbledon Manor House under the Cecils* (1962).

Milward, R.J: *Tudor Wimbledon* (1972).

Milward, R.J: *Wimbledon in the Time of the Civil War* (1976).

Milward, R.J: *Wimbledon's Manor Houses* (1982).

Milward, R.J: *A Georgian Village: Wimbledon, 1724-65* (1986).

Milward, R.J: *Cannizaro House and its Park* (1991).

Milward, R.J: *The Spencers in Wimbledon, 1744-1994* (1996).

Milward, R.J: *Wimbledon Two Hundred Years Ago* (1996).

Potter, G: 'Eagle House, Wimbledon: The Excavation of an early seventeenth century Garden' in *Art and Symbolism in Medieval Europe* (1997).

Strong, R: *The Renaissance Garden in England* (1979).

Victorian and Twentieth Century Wimbledon

Baker, E.C: *Sir William Preece* (1976).

Barrett, J: *A Hundred Wimbledon Championships* (1986).

Copeland, H (editor): *Wimbledon and Merton Annual*: vol. 1 (1903): Eagle House; Wimbledon at the Accession of Queen Victoria; vol. 4 (1910) Old Folks' Memories.

Cornfield, S: *The Queen's Prize: The Story of the N.R.A.* (1987).

Curry, C: *Memories of my side of the Common* (1989).

Elliot, A: *Wimbledon's Railways* (1982).

Fawcett, P: *Memories of a Wimbledon Childhood, 1906-18* (1981).

Hawtin, G: *A new View of old Wimbledon*, vols III and IV (1993).

Milward, R.J: *Portrait of a Church: The Sacred Heart, Wimbledon, 1887-1987* (1987).

Milward, R.J: *Two Wimbledon Roads: Edge Hill and Darlaston Road* (1991).

Milward, R.J: *Wimbledon, Then and Now* (1995).

Milward, R.J: *Wimbledon, 1865-1965* (1997).

Montgomery, J: *The Twenties* (1957).

Norman-Smith, B. and D: *The Grange: A Centenary Portrait* (1984).

Ogley, B: *Surrey at War* (1995).

Parsloe, G: *Wimbledon Village Club and Village Hall, 1858-1958* (1958).

Plastow, N: *Safe as Houses: Wimbledon 1939-45* (1972; 2nd edn 1990).

Plastow, N: *The Wimbledon Windmill* (1977).

Rondeau, B: *Wimbledon Park: From Private Park to Residential Suburb* (1995).

Whitehead, W: *Wimbledon 1885-1965* (1965).

Willis, R: *A History and Guidebook of Christ Church* (1972).

Wilson, C: *London United Tramways* (1971).

Other Sources

At the Wimbledon Society Museum: Borough Guides; Deeds; Memories of John Cloake and Eileen Bowen.

At Merton Local Studies Centre: Directories; Newspapers; Census Returns; Rate books; St Mary's Parish Reports.